Hello
I'M TKAII BATTS

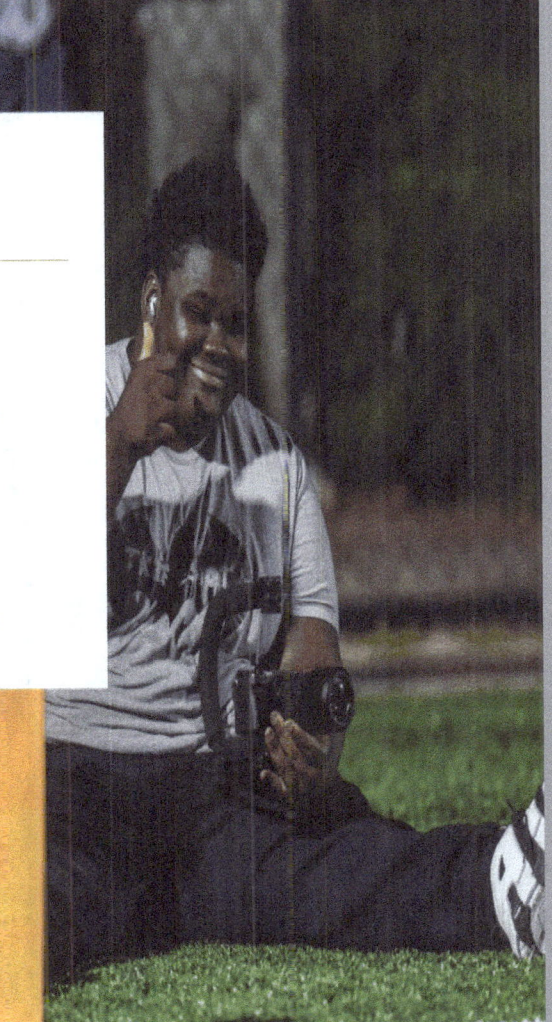

PHOTOGRAPHER/ VIDEOGRAPHER

My name is Tkaii Batts, a 19 year old photographer and videographer with a passion for showing others that if you believe in yourself, you can achieve anything. This book is here to guide you on how to start photography the right way and help you grow your skills to levels you never thought possible.

@Tk2eyeshot - all socials

THE ART OF SPORT PHOTOGRAPHY

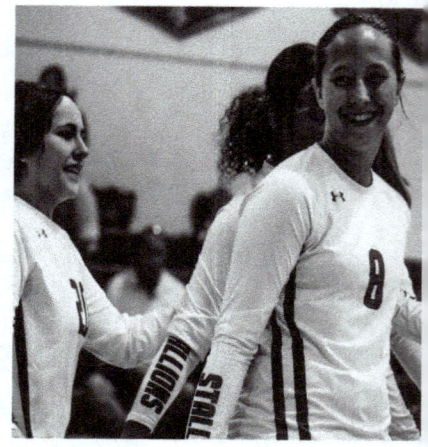

Photography is more than just capturing images; it's an art form that requires a blend of technical skill, creativity, and timing. Each shot tells a unique story, capturing fleeting moments and emotions that can resonate deeply with viewers. The magic lies in understanding not only the mechanics of a camera but also the nuances of light, composition, and movement. With these elements in harmony, even a simple image can evoke powerful feelings or transport someone into a different moment entirely.

Passion is the fuel that can elevate photography to an extraordinary level. When you're truly passionate about photography, every opportunity becomes a learning experience, and each picture becomes a canvas. This drive pushes you to experiment, refine, and develop your unique style. With this kind of dedication, your skills can reach heights you may not have imagined, as passion brings out the commitment to consistently improve, making the art of photography both personal and boundless in possibility.

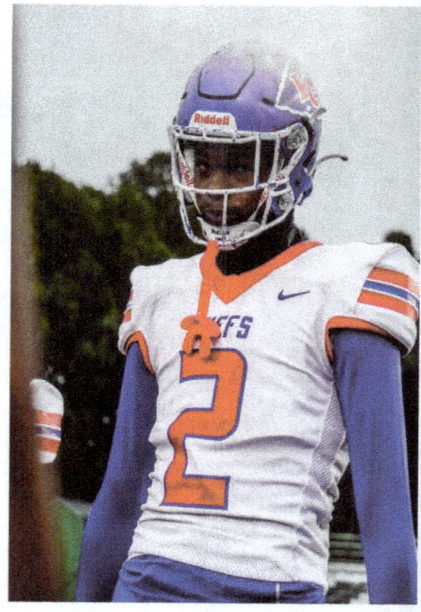

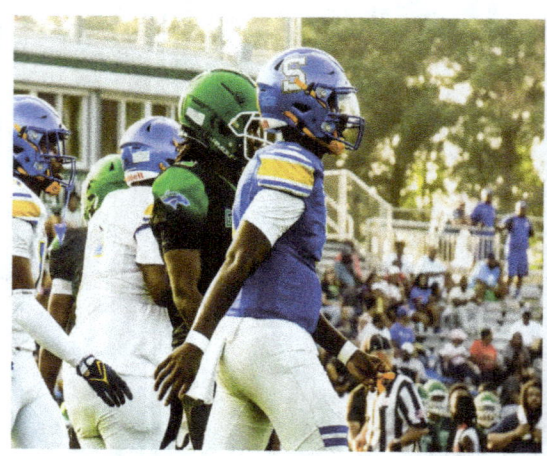

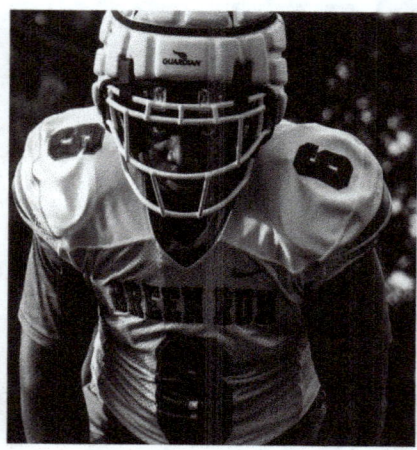

Photographer
Essential 101

what do I need to start sports photography

For sports photography, the right equipment is essential, but you don't need to break the bank to get started. A budget-friendly DSLR or mirrorless camera like the Canon T7 or Sony a6700 will offer high-speed continuous shooting and quick autofocus to keep up with fast action. Pair this with a more affordable telephoto lens, such as a 55-128mm, which works well for beginners. A 128GB SanDisk memory card (V60-rated for high-resolution cameras) ensures ample storage and reliable performance. Additional essentials include a monopod for stability, extra batteries, and a rain cover to protect your gear. With this setup, you'll be ready to capture the excitement of sports with clarity and impact.

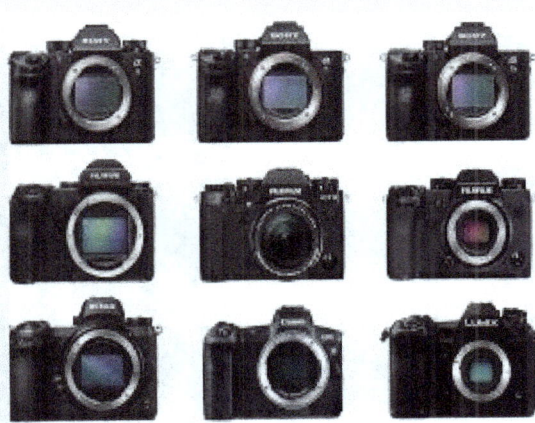

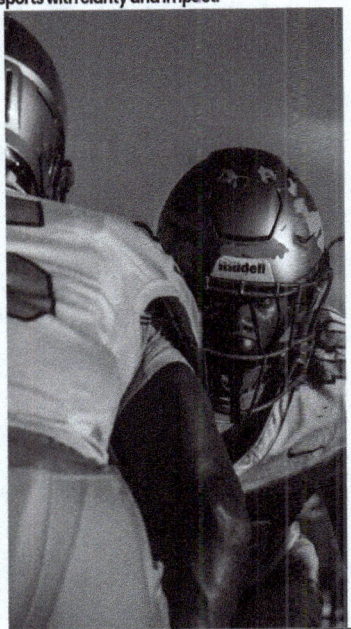

what's missing?

Having a dedicated camera bag is crucial to keep all your gear organized and easily accessible, from your camera and lenses to memory cards and extra batteries. Don't forget your phone it's a powerful tool for on-the go editing. You don't always need a laptop or PC to refine your photos. Free apps like CapCut, PicsArt, Canva, and Lightroom are essential for editing and can help you enhance your images anytime, anywhere, making them a must have for any photographer.

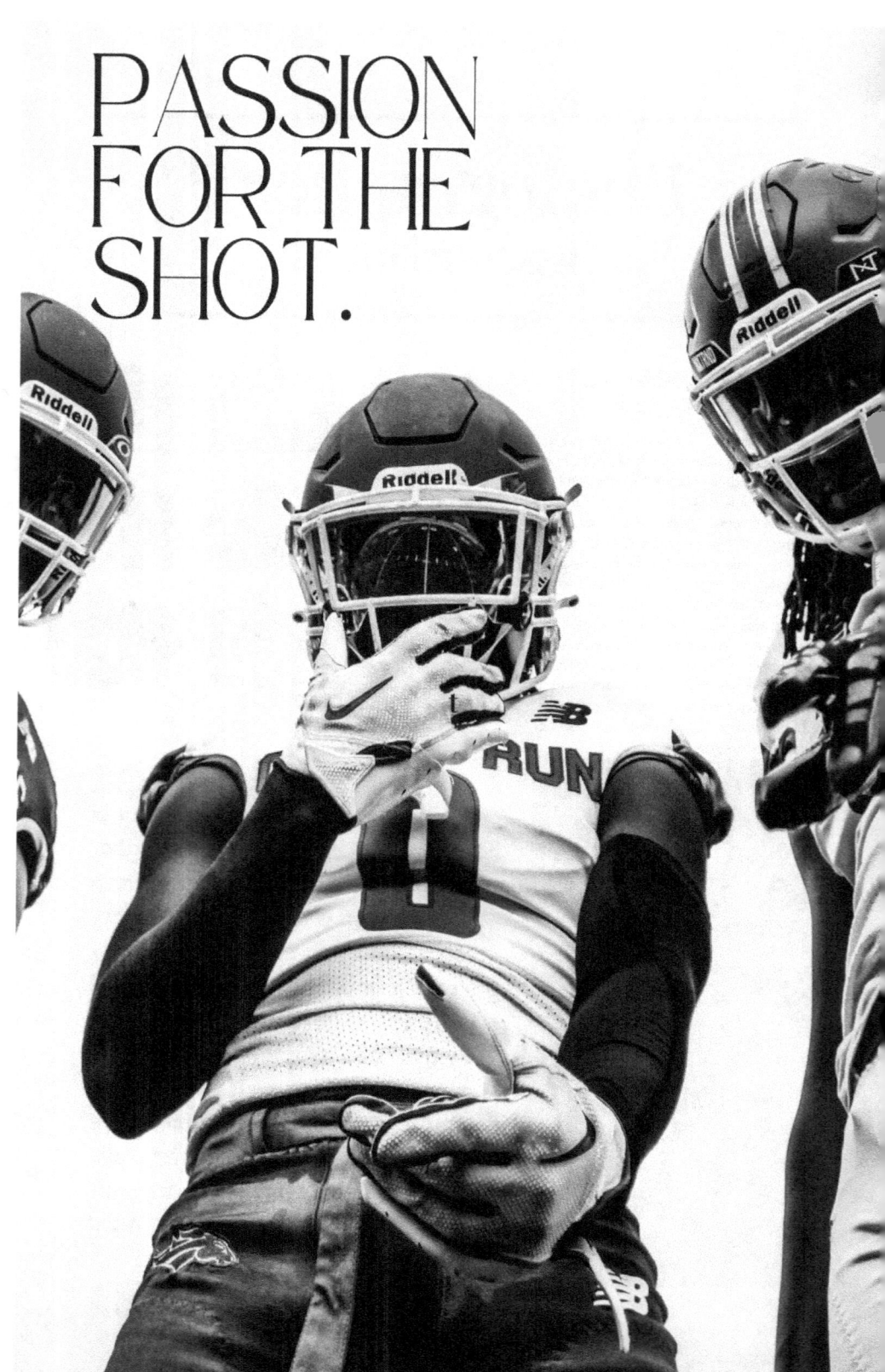

PASSION
FOR THE
SHOT.

POSITIONING
AND
LOCATION

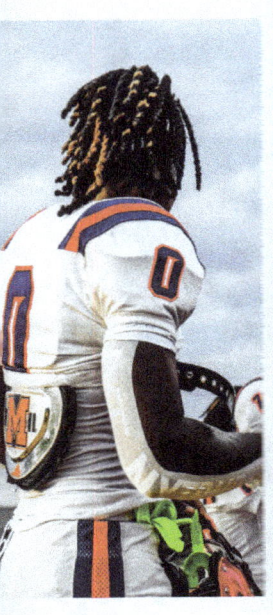
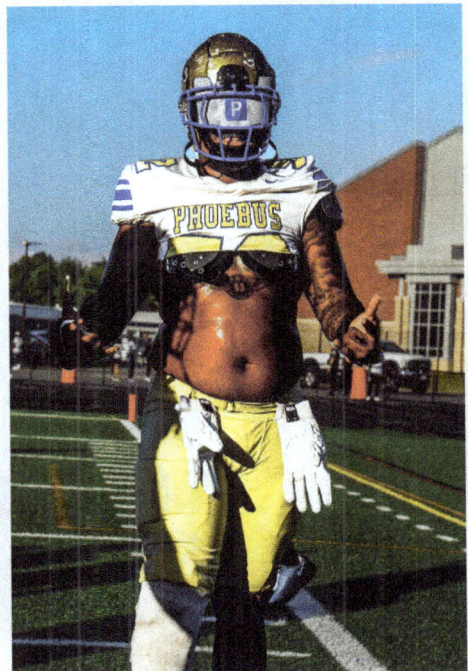

WHAT SHOULD DO ?

Anticipating where the action will happen is crucial for capturing impactful shots. In basketball, positioning yourself under the basket is ideal for close-ups of layups, dunks, and rebounds. For football, align yourself along the sideline to capture the intensity of players in motion. Always face the offense as they move down the field to catch pivotal moments, and position yourself on the side opposite the quarterback's throwing arm to get a clear view of their face and the play's development.

Exploring different angles adds variety and energy to your sports photography. Low angles emphasize the power and intensity of athletes, making them appear larger than life, while high angles provide a strategic overview of the game, showcasing formations and team dynamics. In football, using these techniques alongside proper positioning ensures you're ready to capture every thrilling moment as it unfolds.

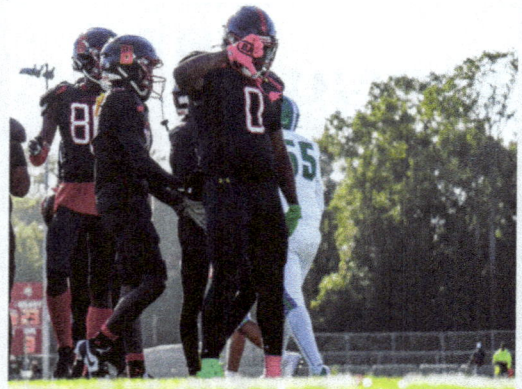

study your subjects

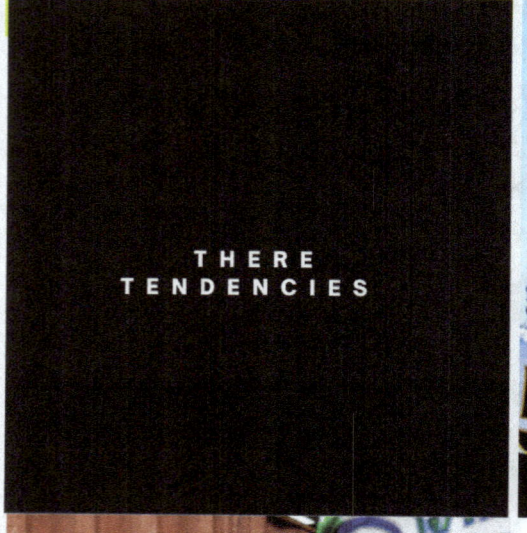

THERE
TENDENCIES

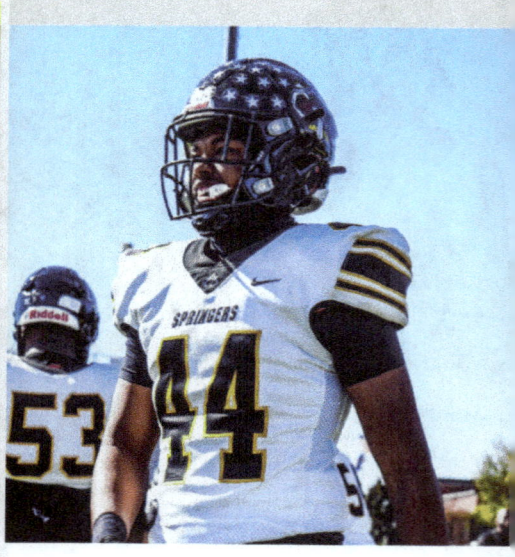

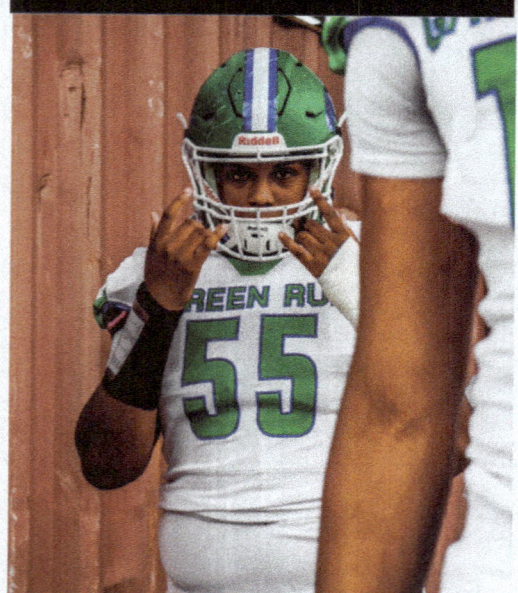

KNOW THERE NEXT
MOVE BEFORE THEY
DO IT,CAPTURE
MOMENT

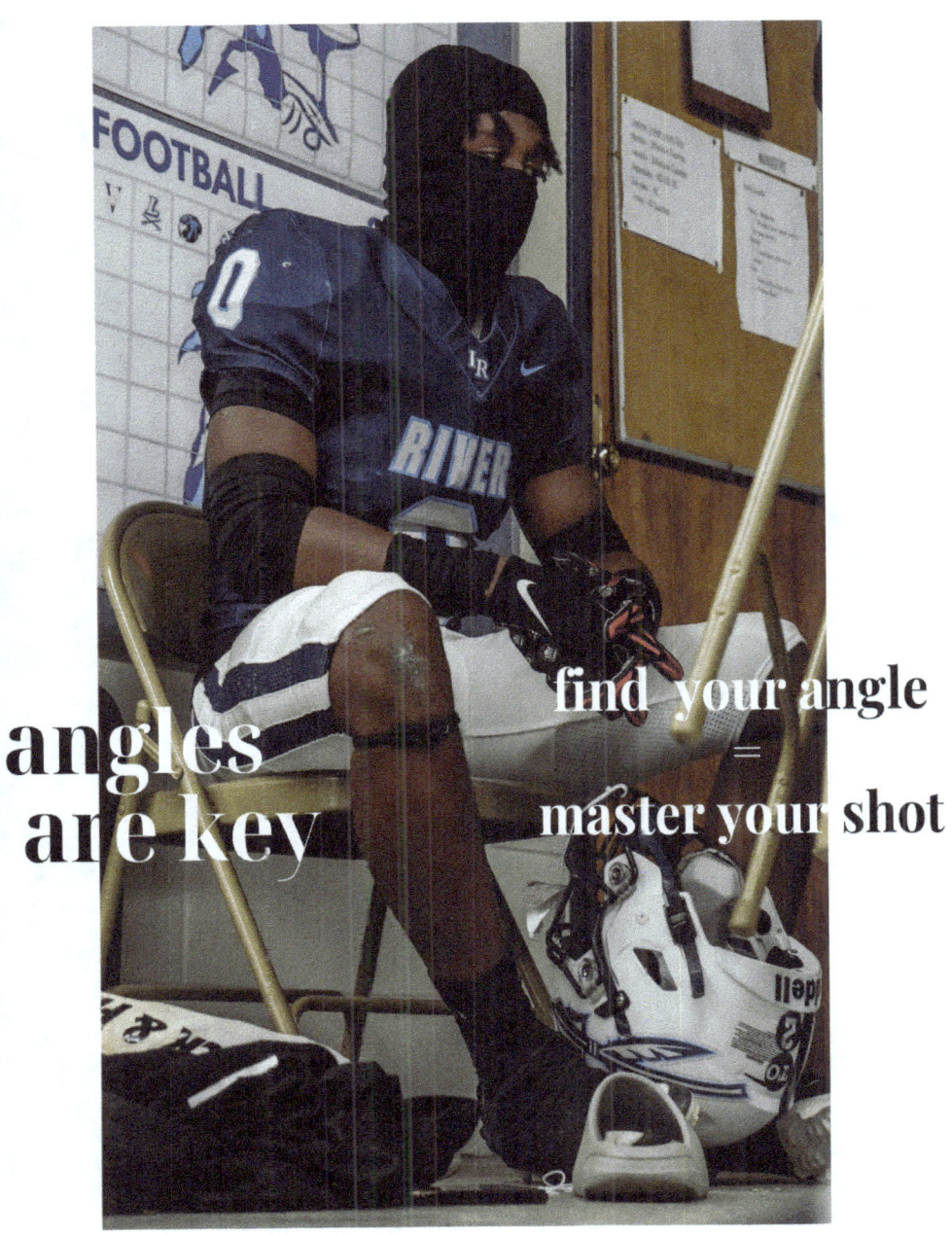

**angles
are key**

**find your angle
=
master your shot**

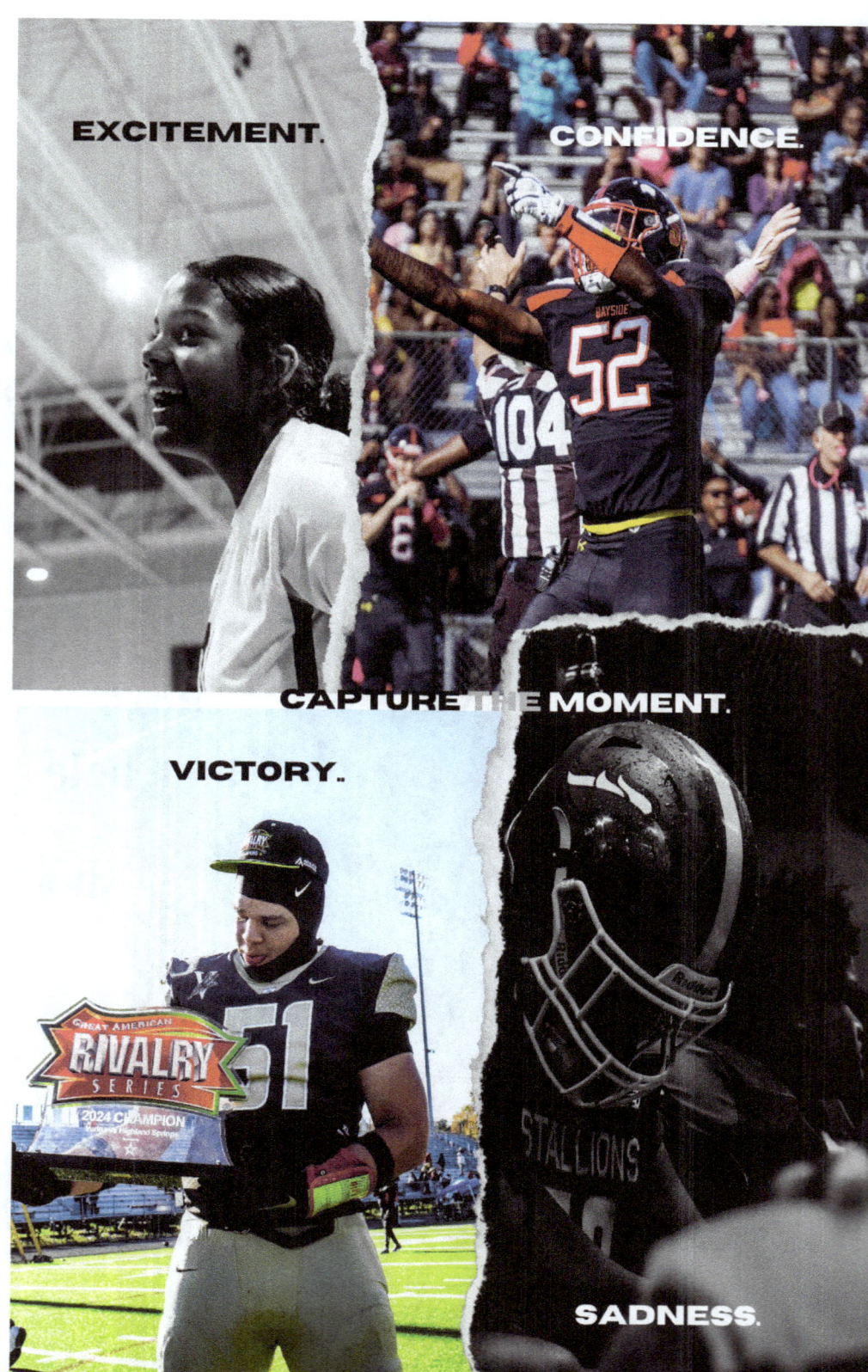

EXCITEMENT.

CONFIDENCE.

CAPTURE THE MOMENT.

VICTORY.

SADNESS.

EXPRESSION

SHOTS

MATTER

SHOW THEIR STORY.

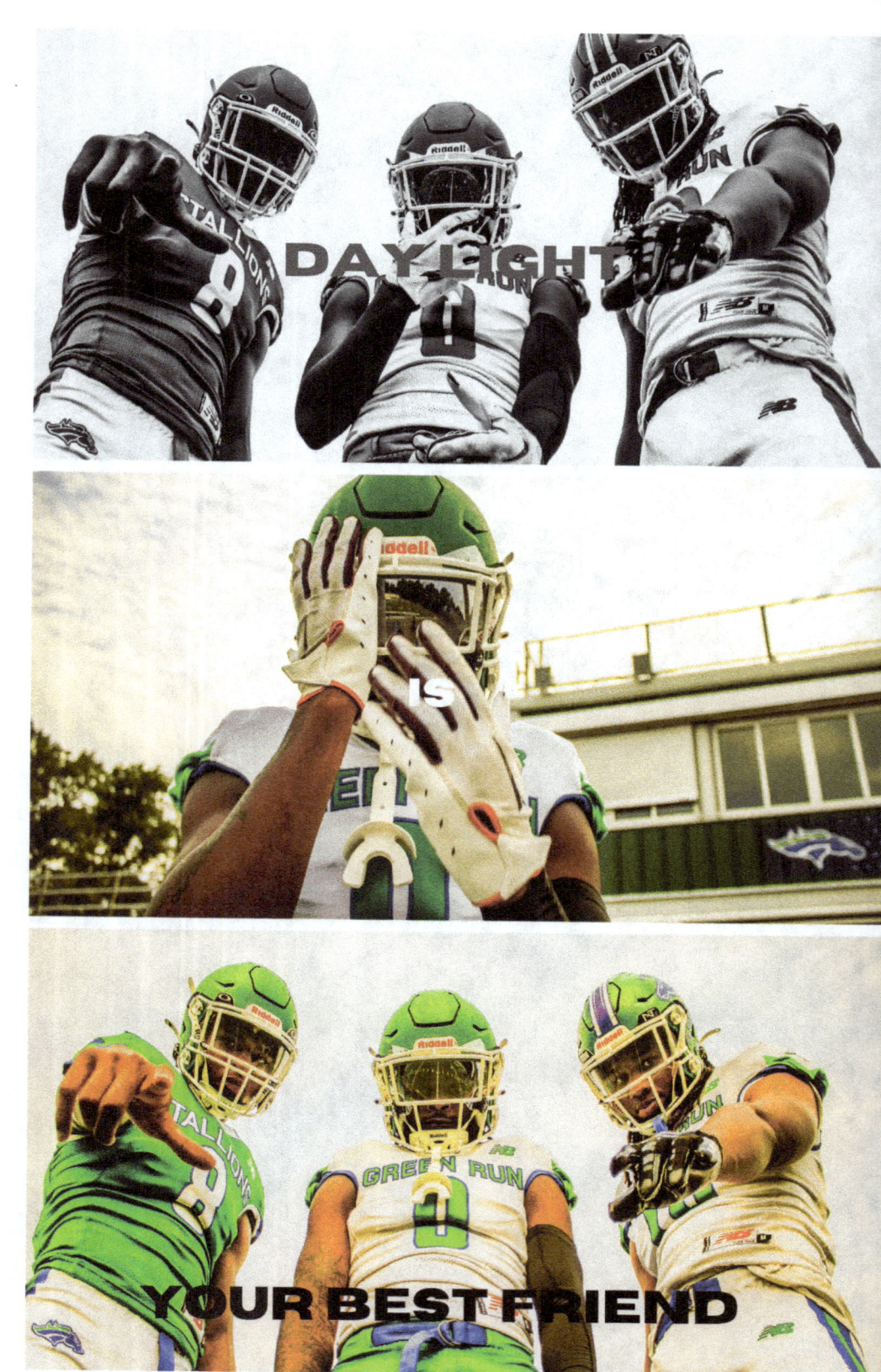

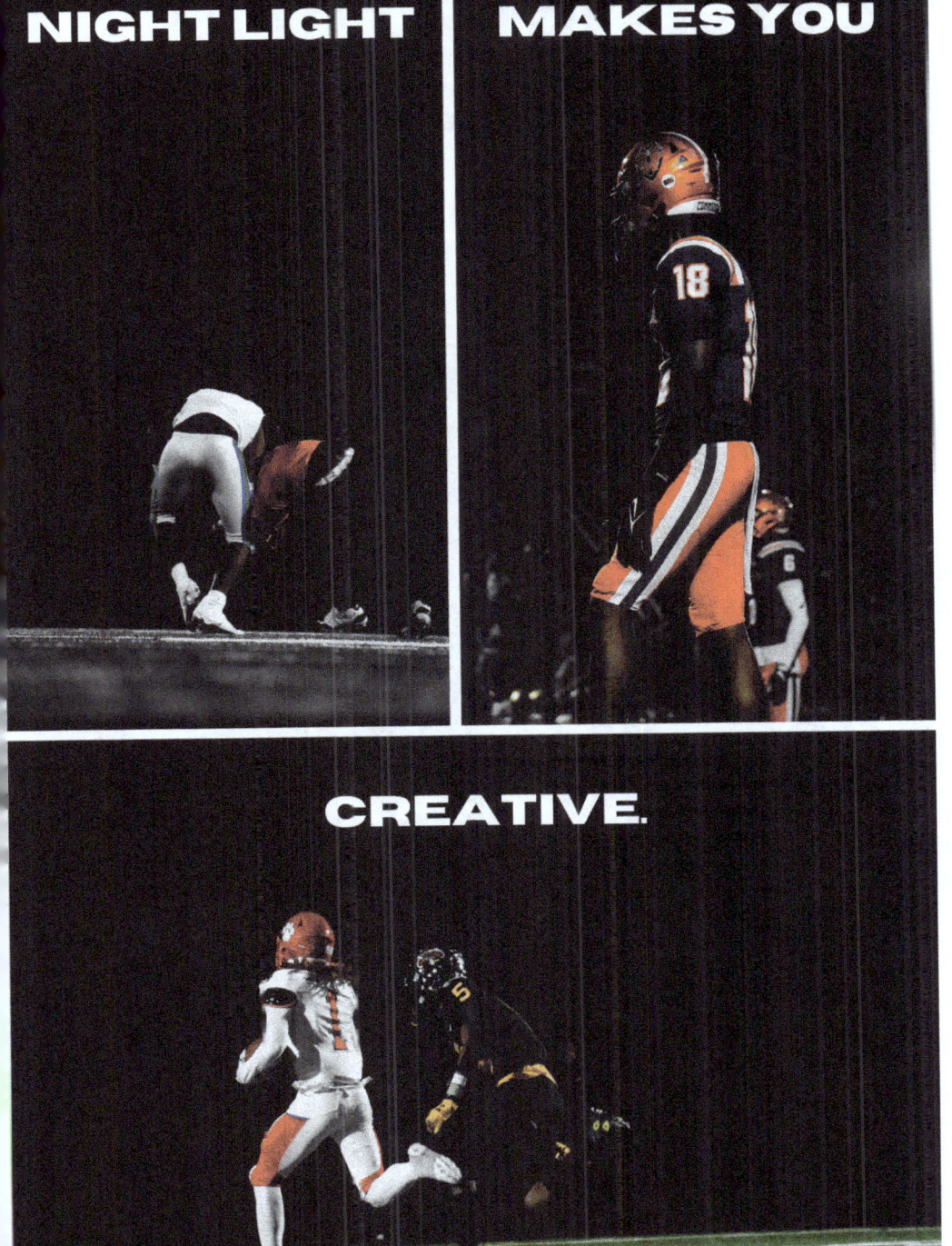

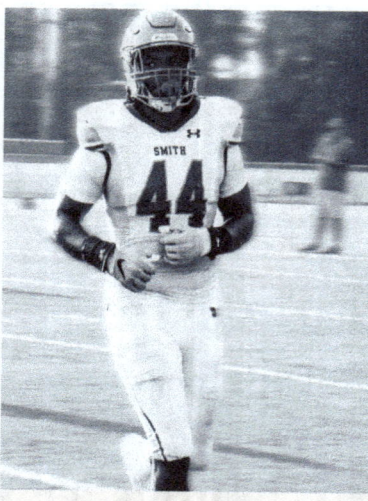

MOTION BLUR EDITING

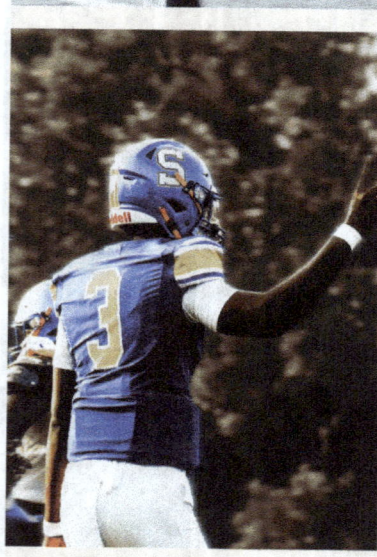

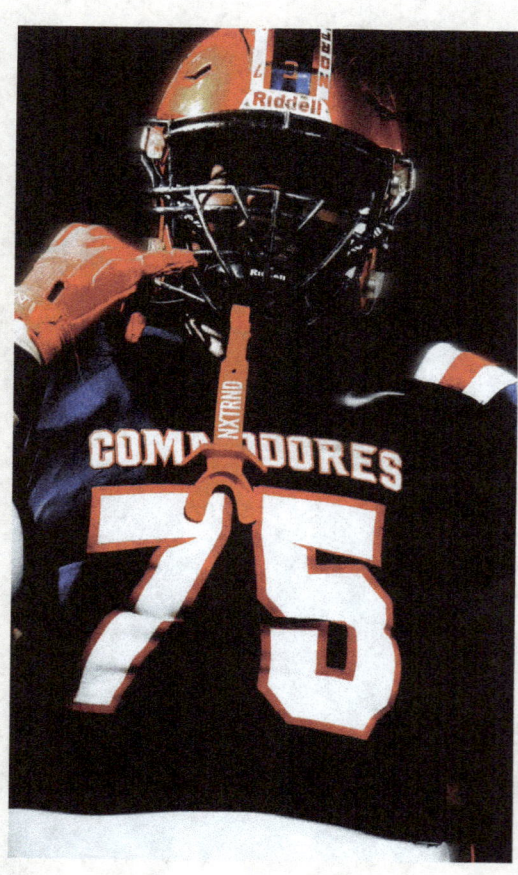

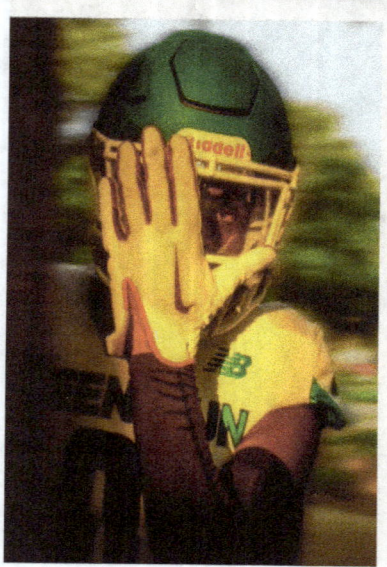

apps like Prequel, CapCut, and PicsArt can significantly enhance your editing skills and foster creativity in photography. These tools provide user friendly interfaces and advanced features, enabling you to experiment with unique effects, transitions, and adjustments. Incorporating such apps into your workflow allows you to refine your photos, develop a distinctive style, and elevate the overall quality of your work, all while exploring new creative possibilities.

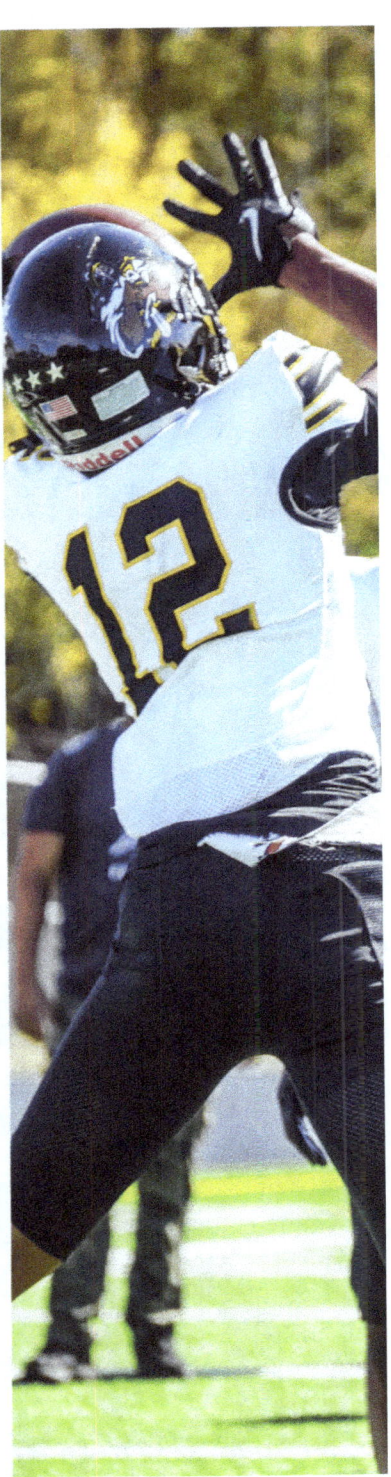

ONE THING YOU
NEED IS
LIGHT‑ROOM

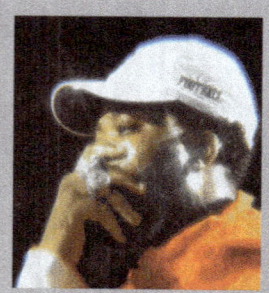

When starting out in photography, studying the work of other photographers can be incredibly valuable. Analyze their styles, compositions, and techniques to understand what makes their work stand out. Once you've learned from their approach, try incorporating elements into your own work, adding your personal twist to create a unique style. Experiment with different environments, lighting, and subjects to refine your skills and discover what excites you. This process of learning, practicing, and experimenting will help you develop your own voice as a photographer, setting you on the path to finding your first paid clients.

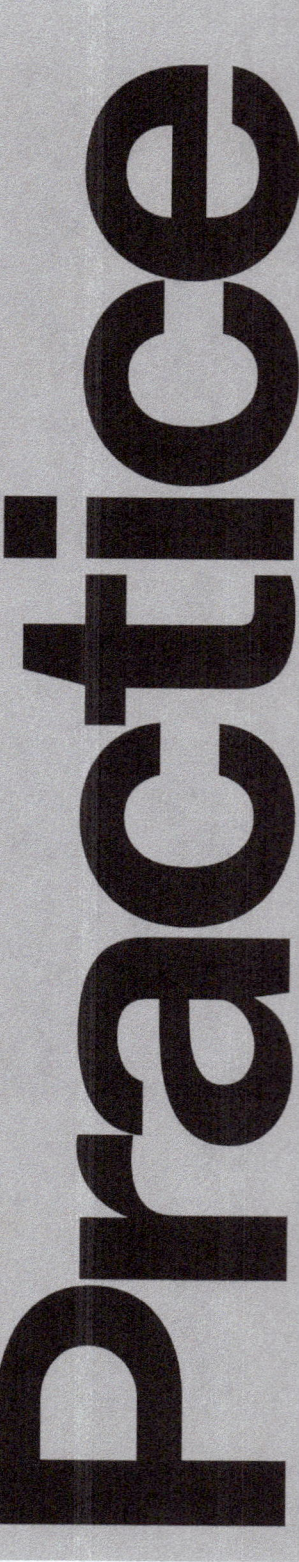

Practice

your story

How can I grow my social media as a photographer?

GROWING YOUR INSTAGRAM AS A PHOTOGRAPHER REQUIRES A COMBINATION OF CONSISTENCY, DEDICATION, AND CREATIVITY. REGULARLY POSTING HIGH-QUALITY CONTENT IS KEY TO KEEPING YOUR AUDIENCE ENGAGED AND ATTRACTING NEW FOLLOWERS. FOCUS ON SHOWCASING YOUR UNIQUE STYLE AND EXPERIMENTING WITH CREATIVE IDEAS TO STAND OUT IN A CROWDED SPACE. HARD WORK IS JUST AS IMPORTANT—ENGAGE WITH YOUR AUDIENCE BY RESPONDING TO COMMENTS, INTERACTING WITH OTHER ACCOUNTS, AND USING RELEVANT HASHTAGS TO INCREASE YOUR REACH. WITH A CONSISTENT POSTING SCHEDULE, THOUGHTFUL INTERACTIONS, AND A CREATIVE APPROACH, YOU CAN STEADILY BUILD A STRONG PRESENCE AND GROW YOUR PLATFORM EFFECTIVELY.

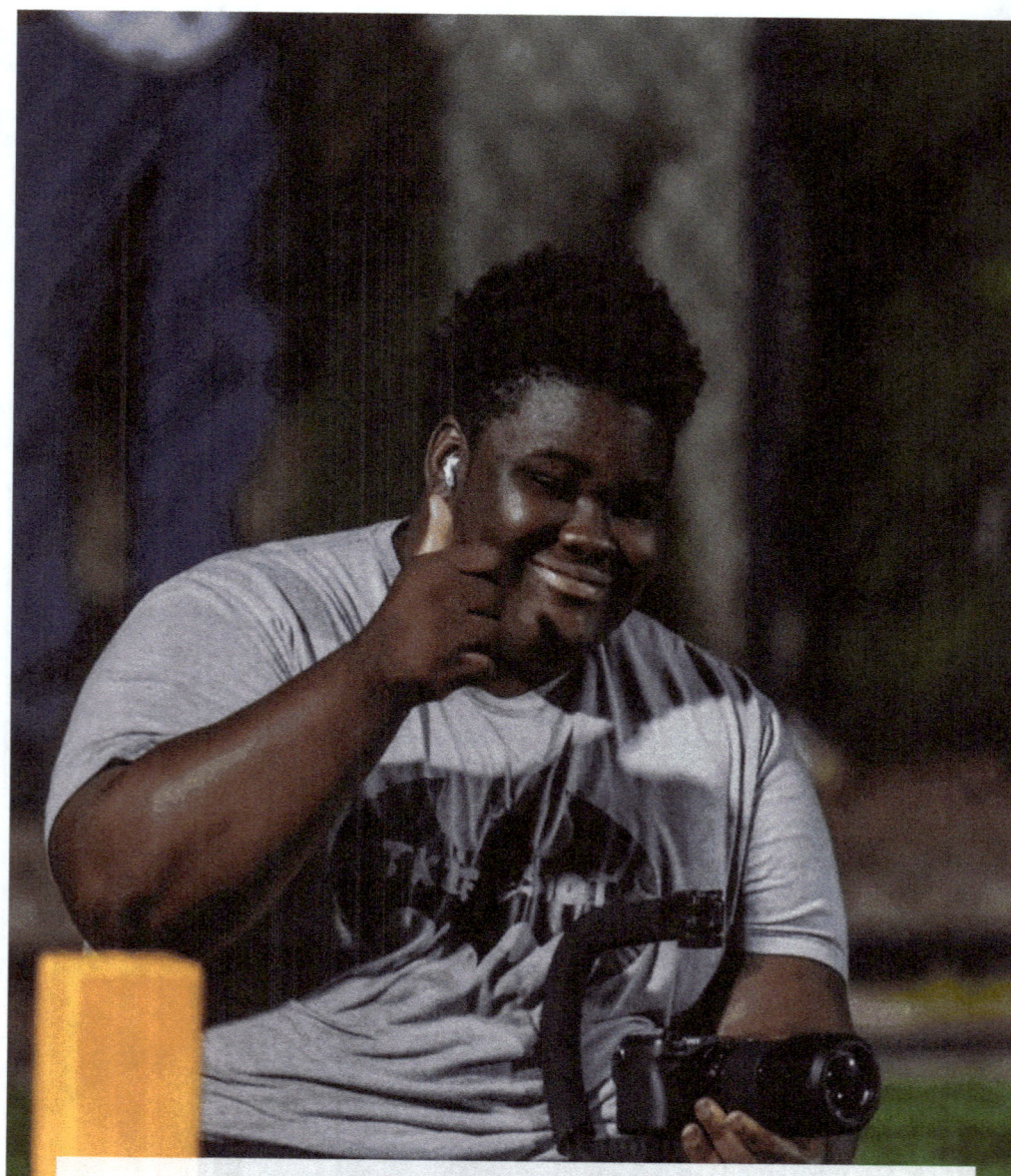

HOW TO FIND ME FOR QUESTION

TKAII BATTS

PHOTOGRAPHY/ VIDEOGRAPHY

@TK2EYESHOT - ON ALL SOICALS

MY PORTFOLIO

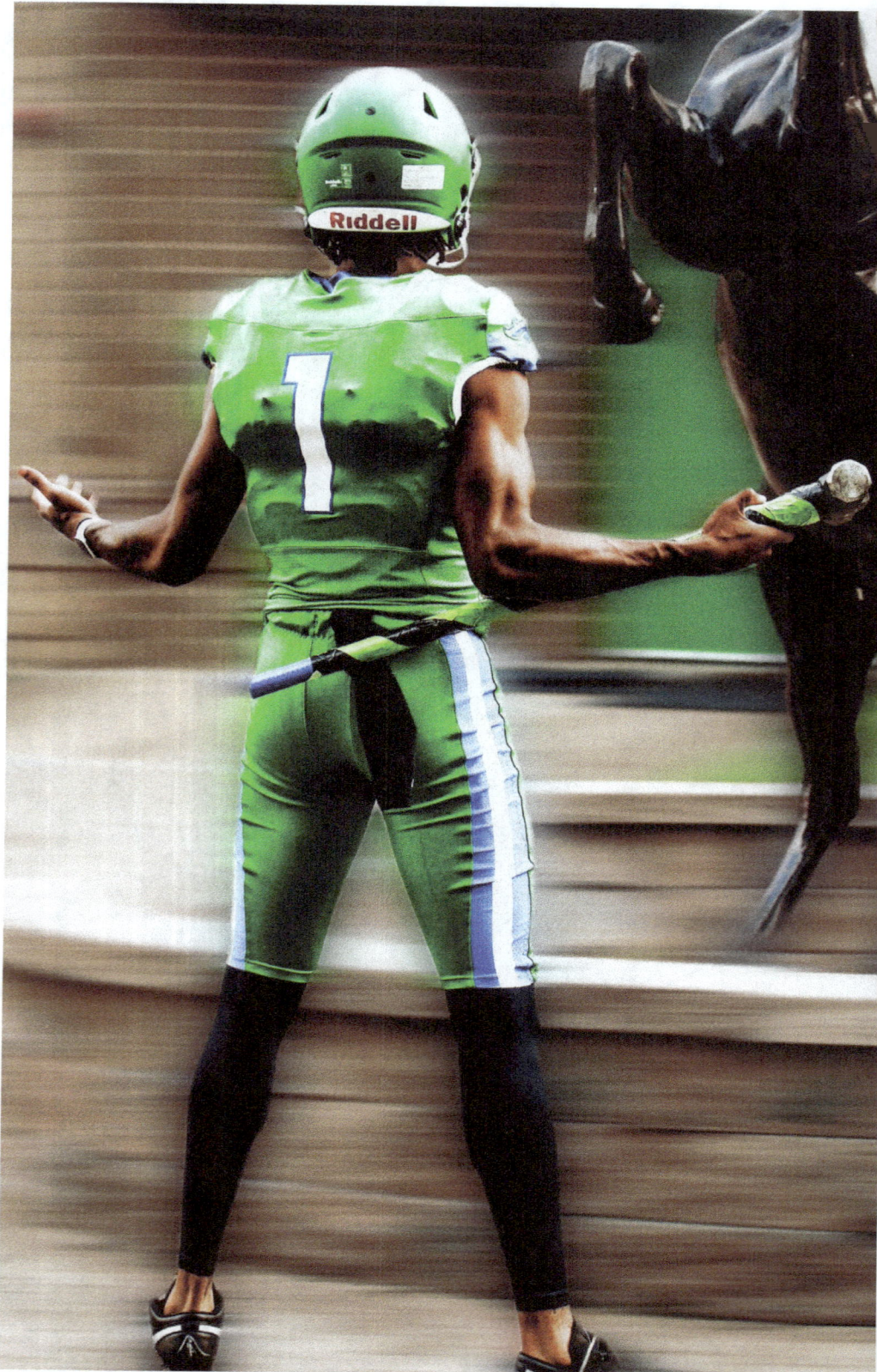

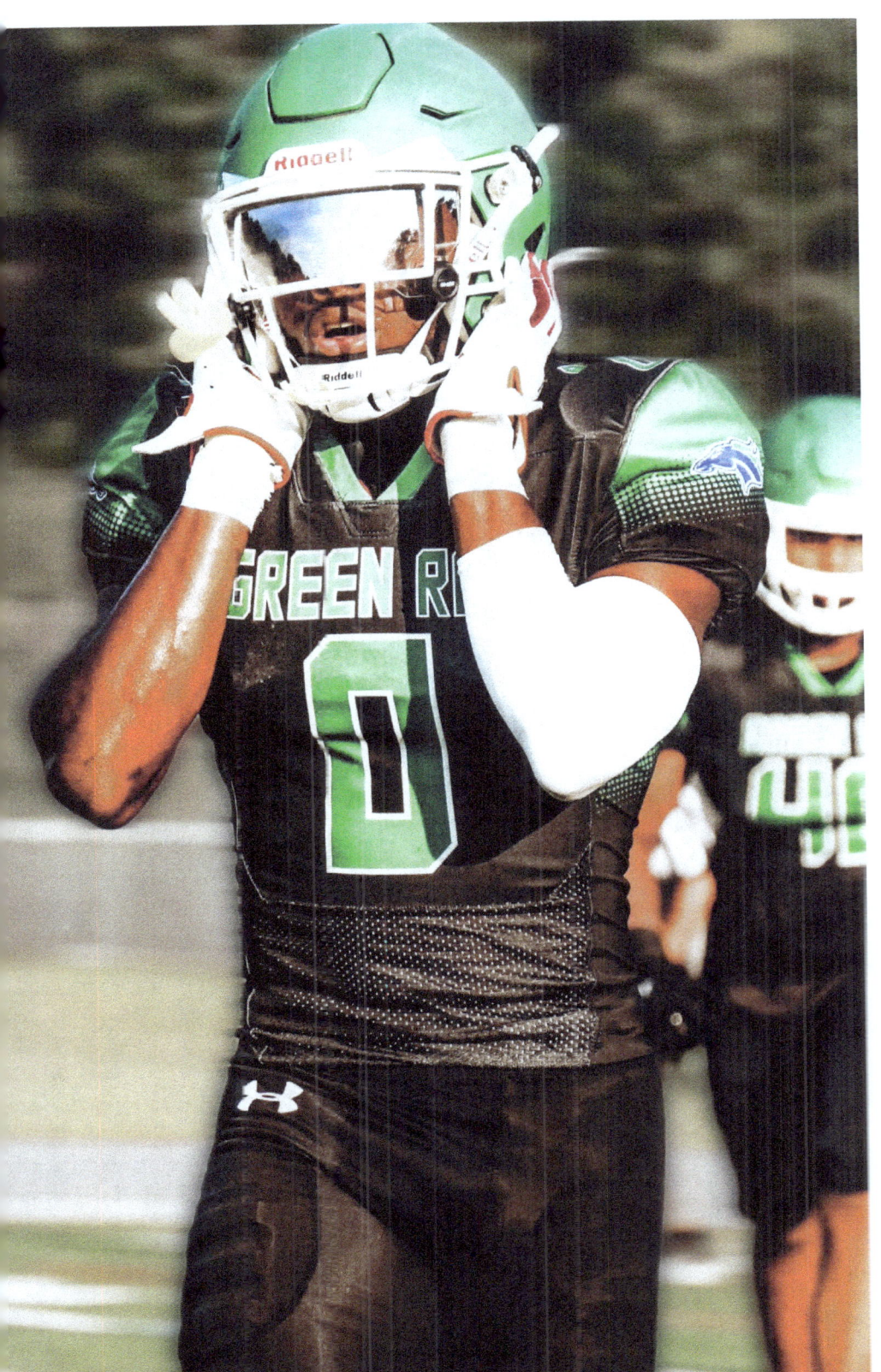

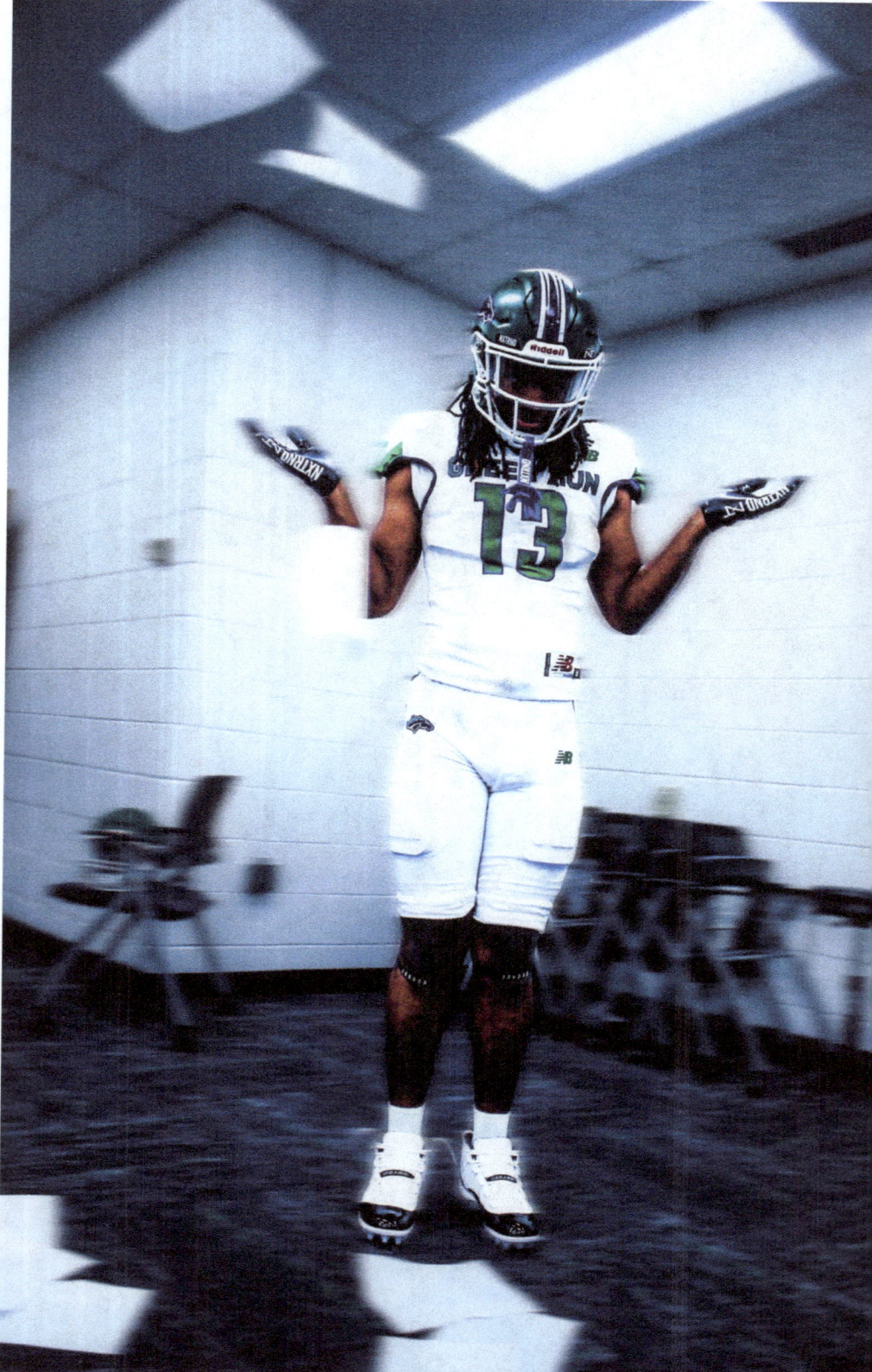

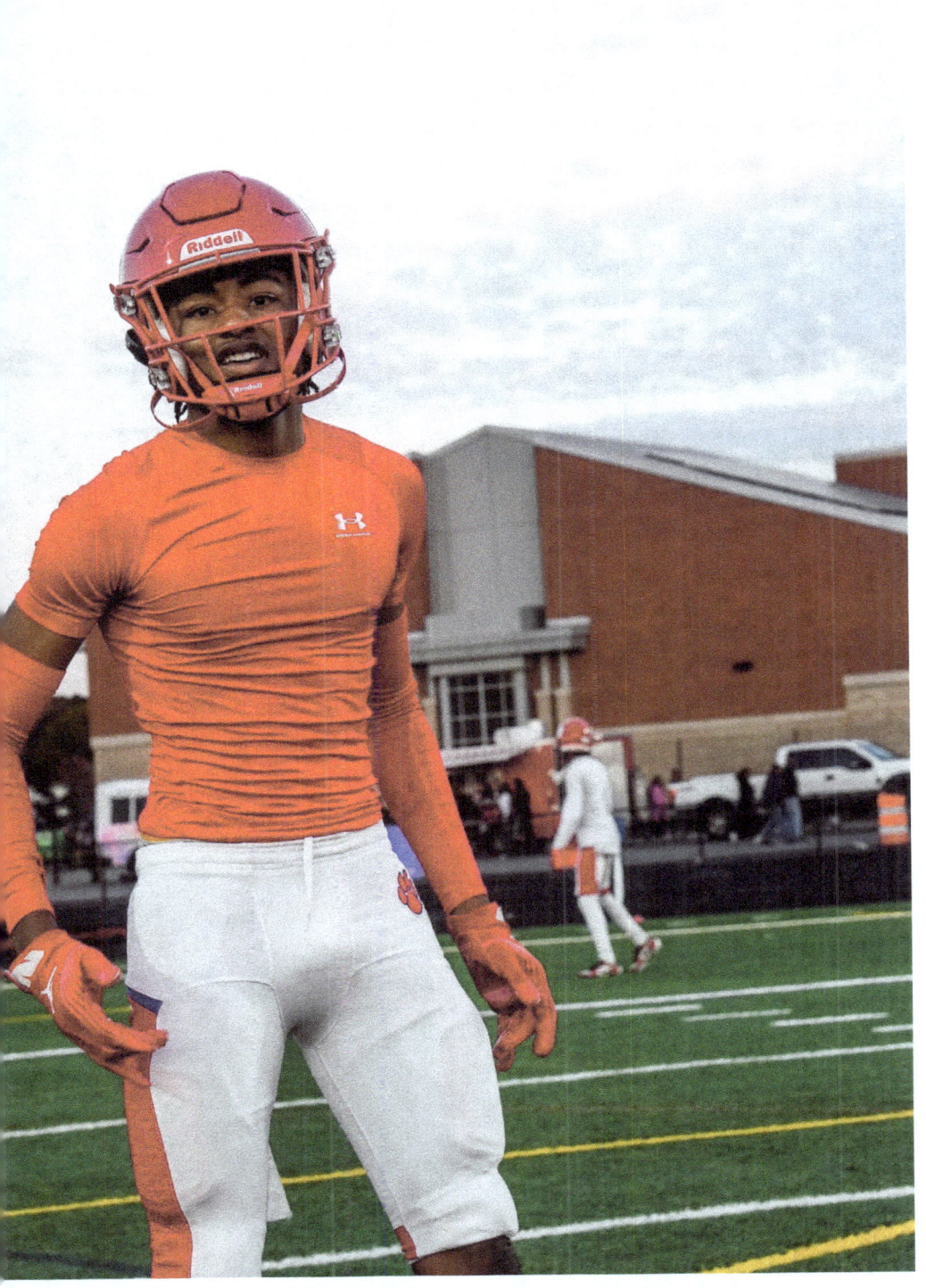

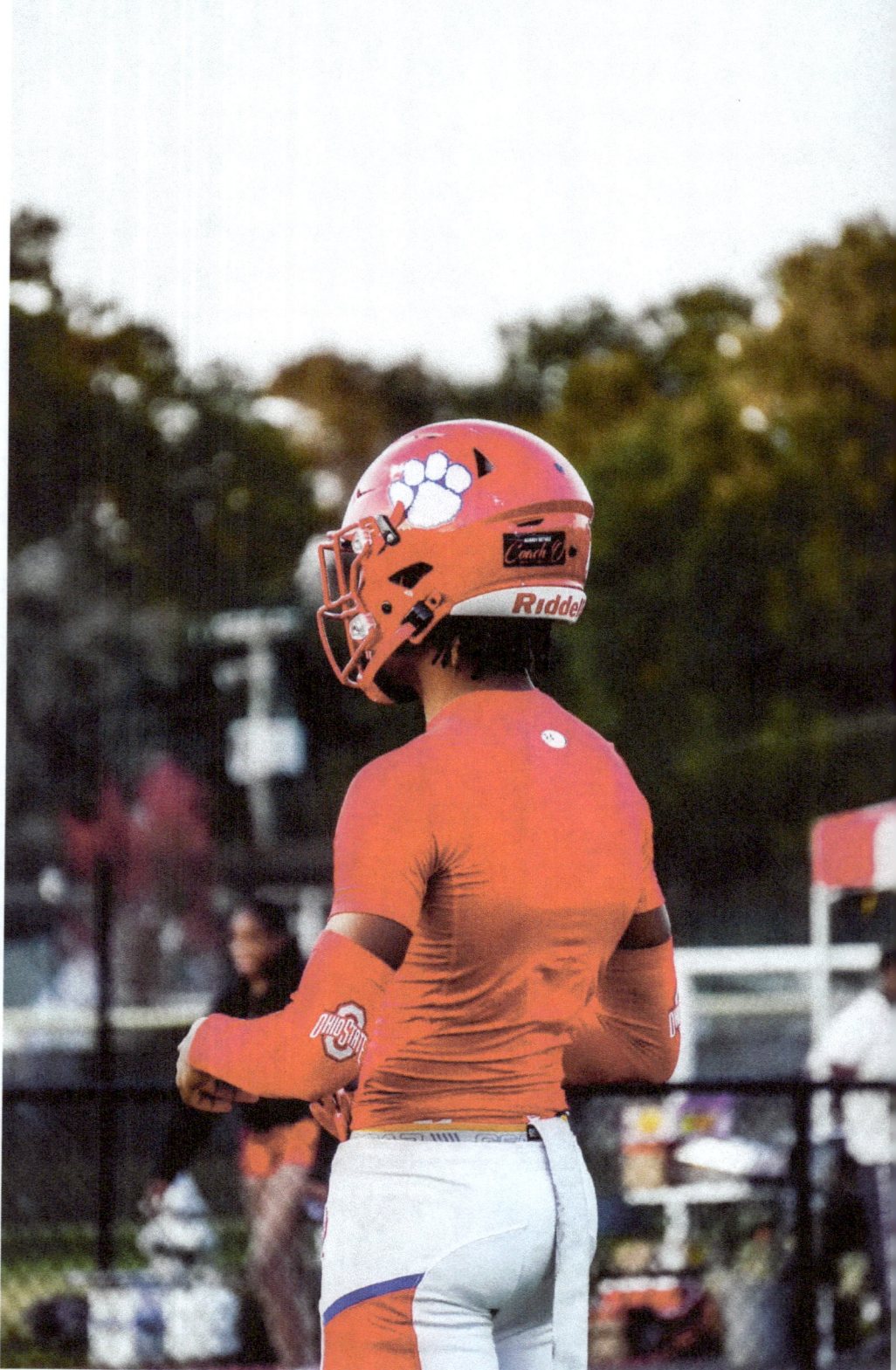

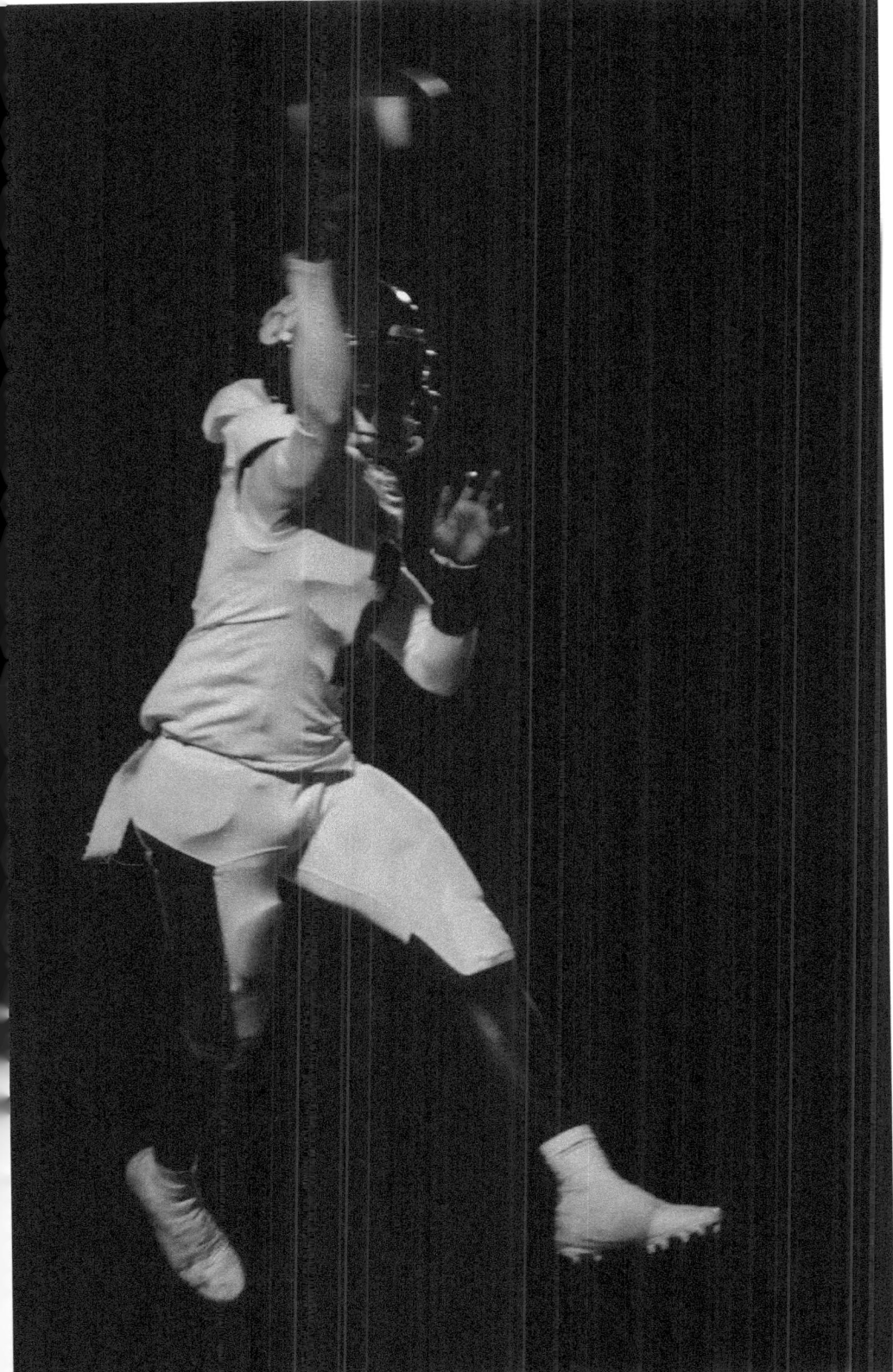

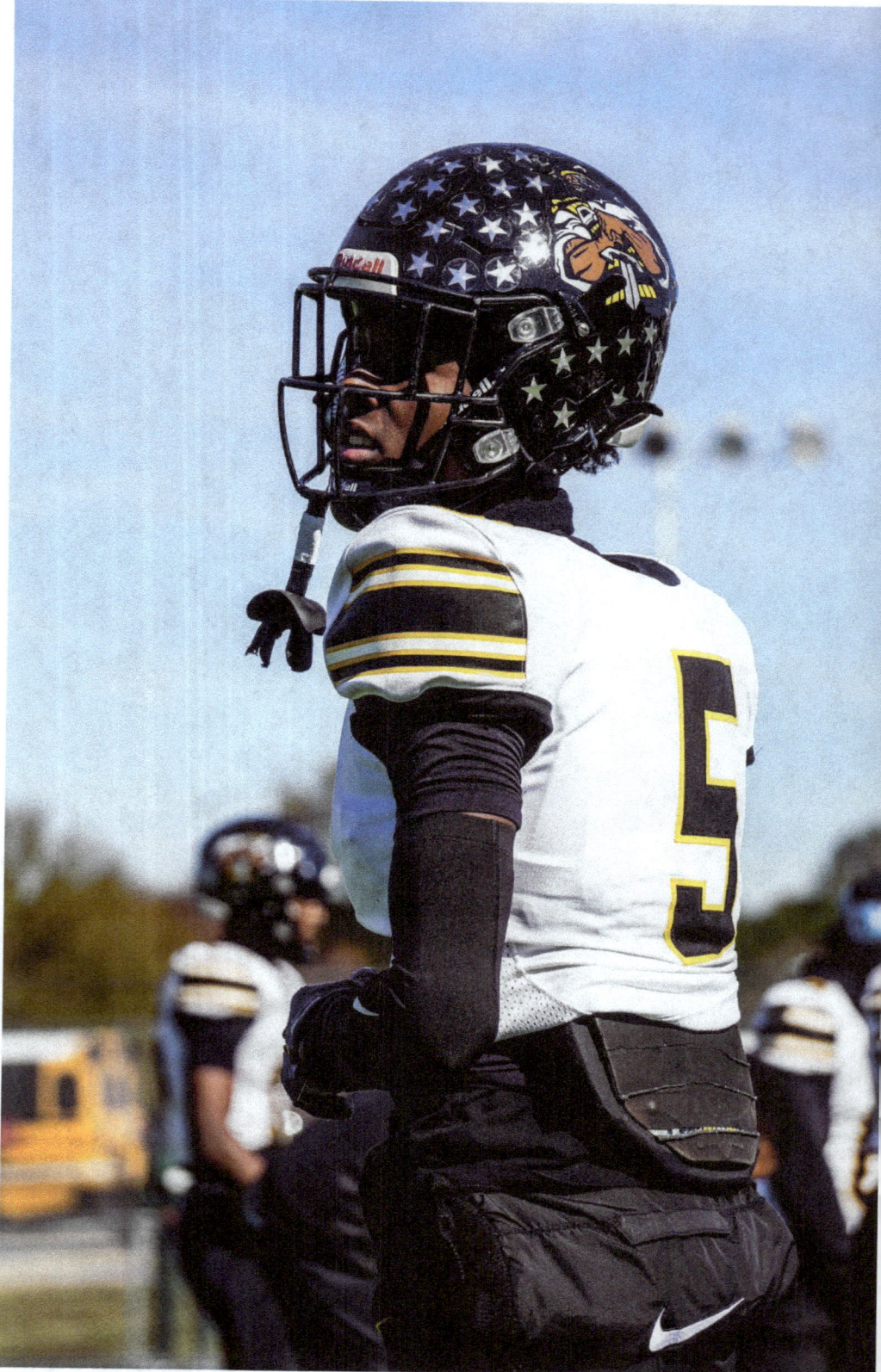

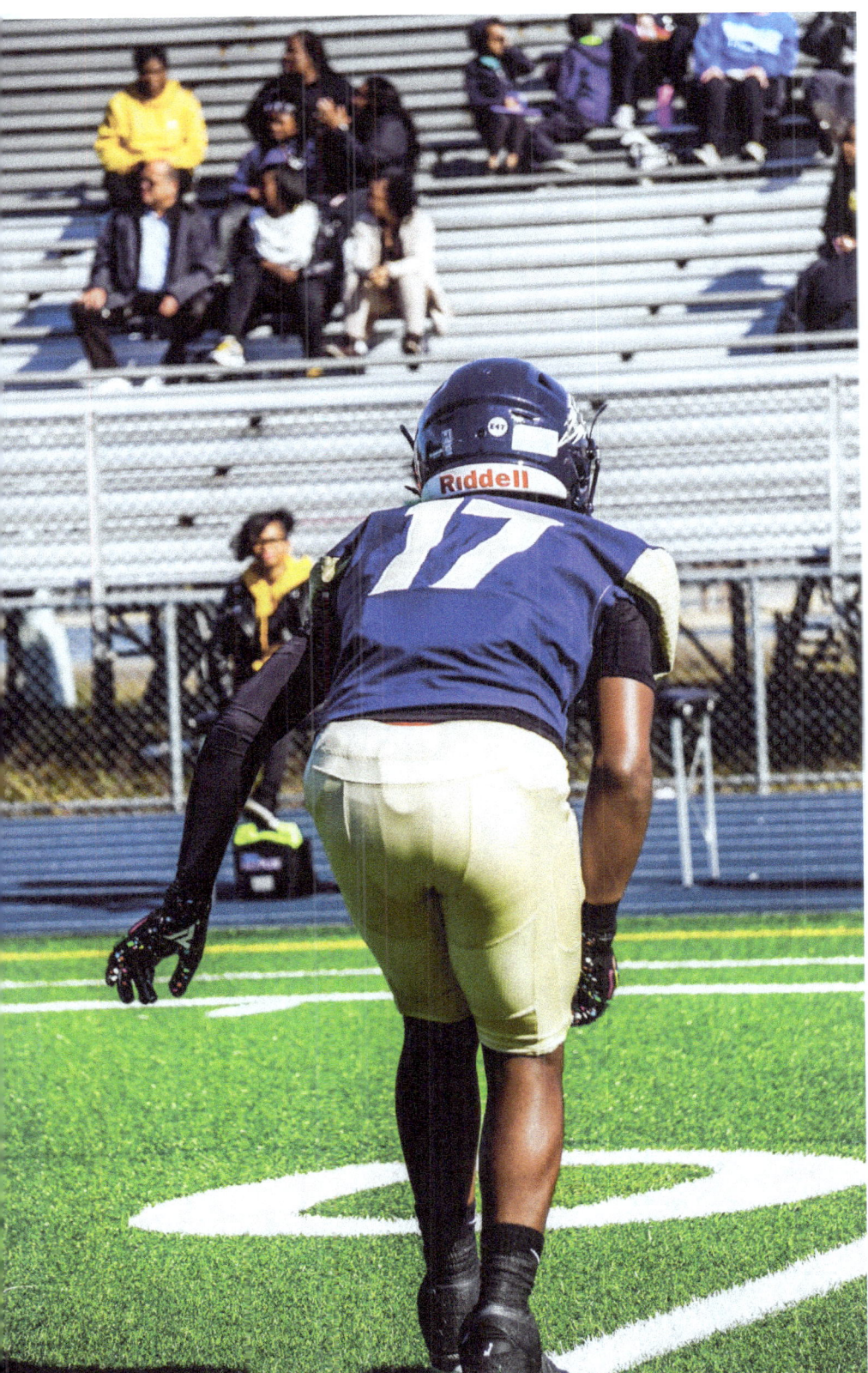

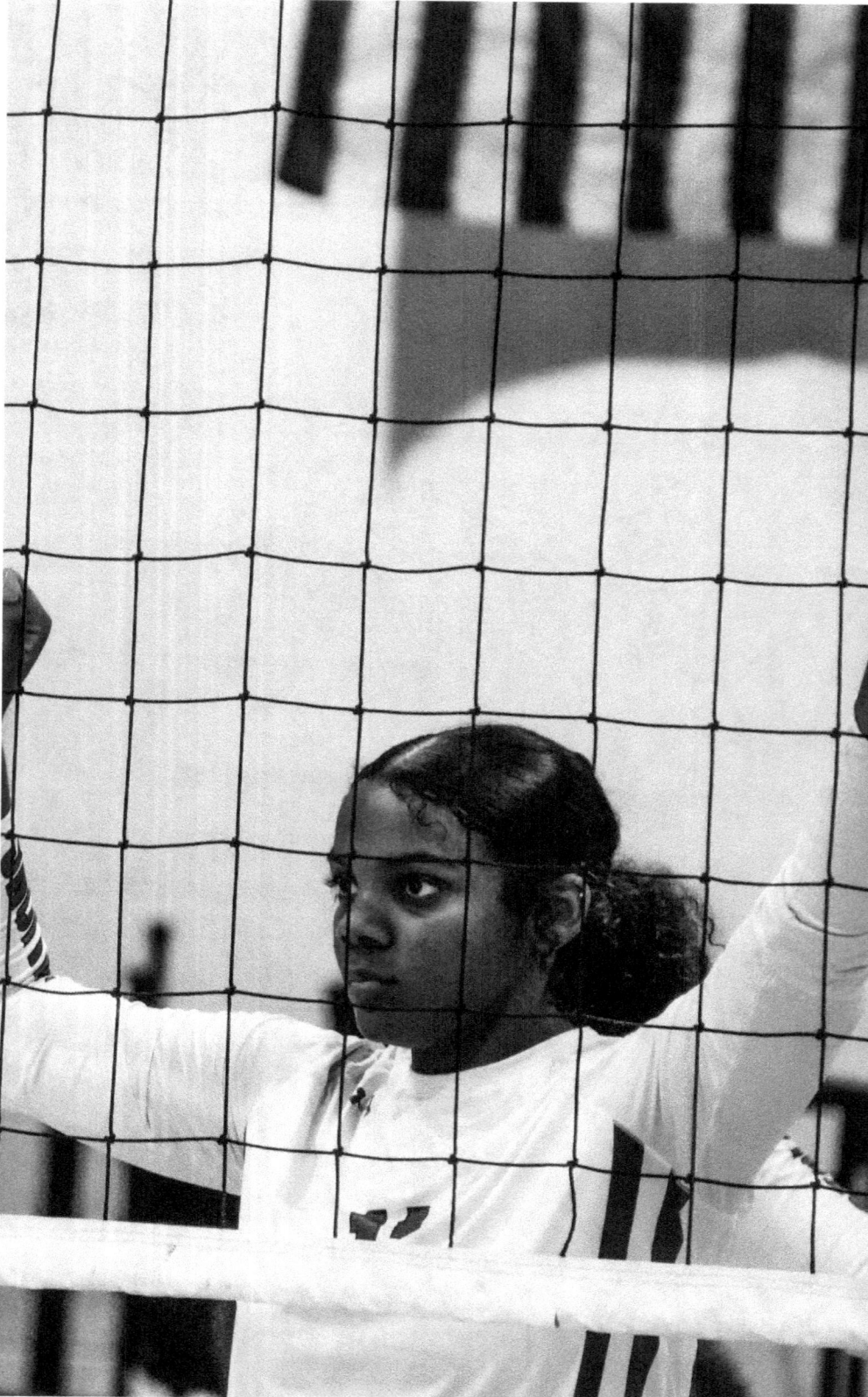

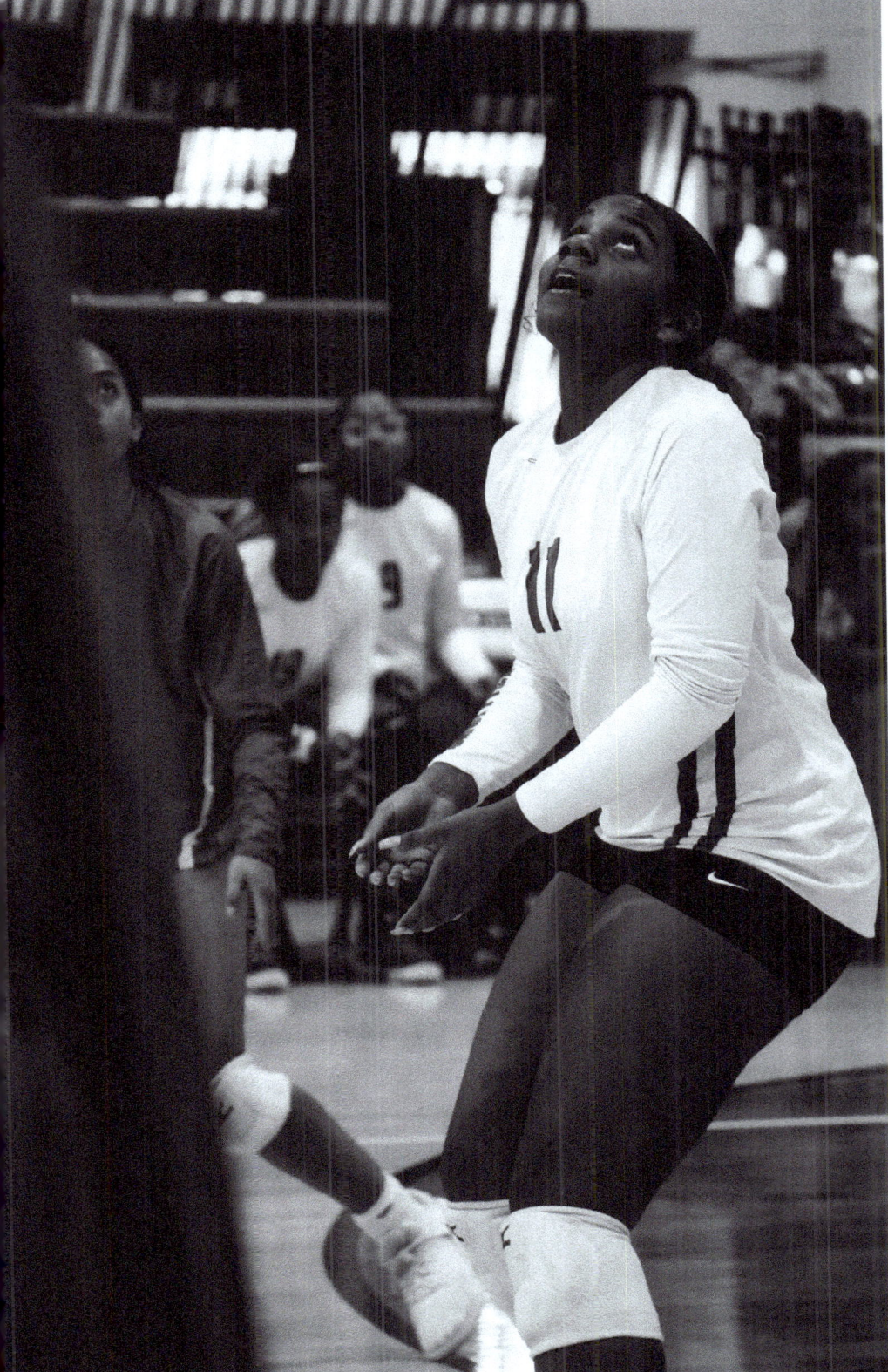

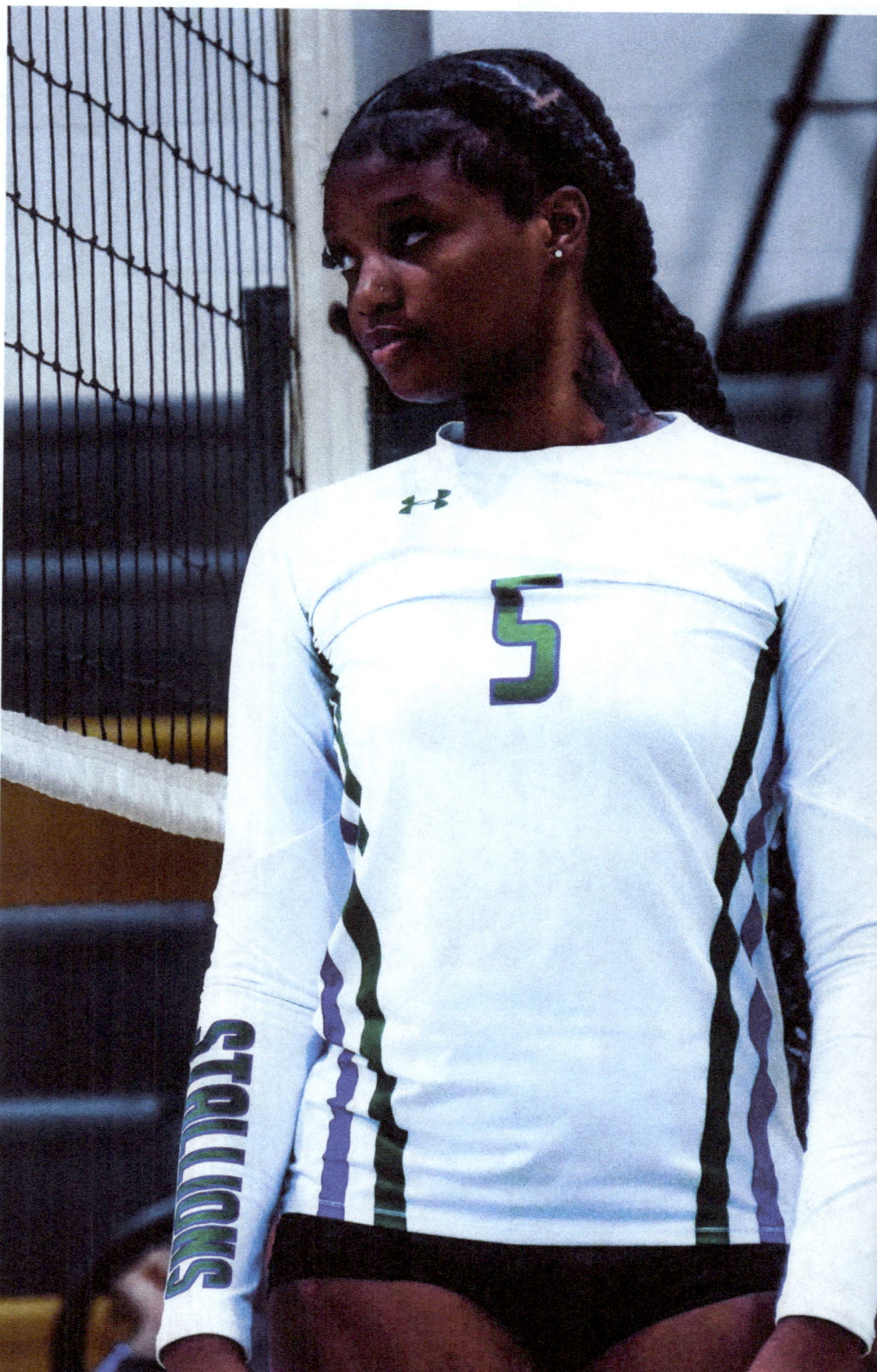

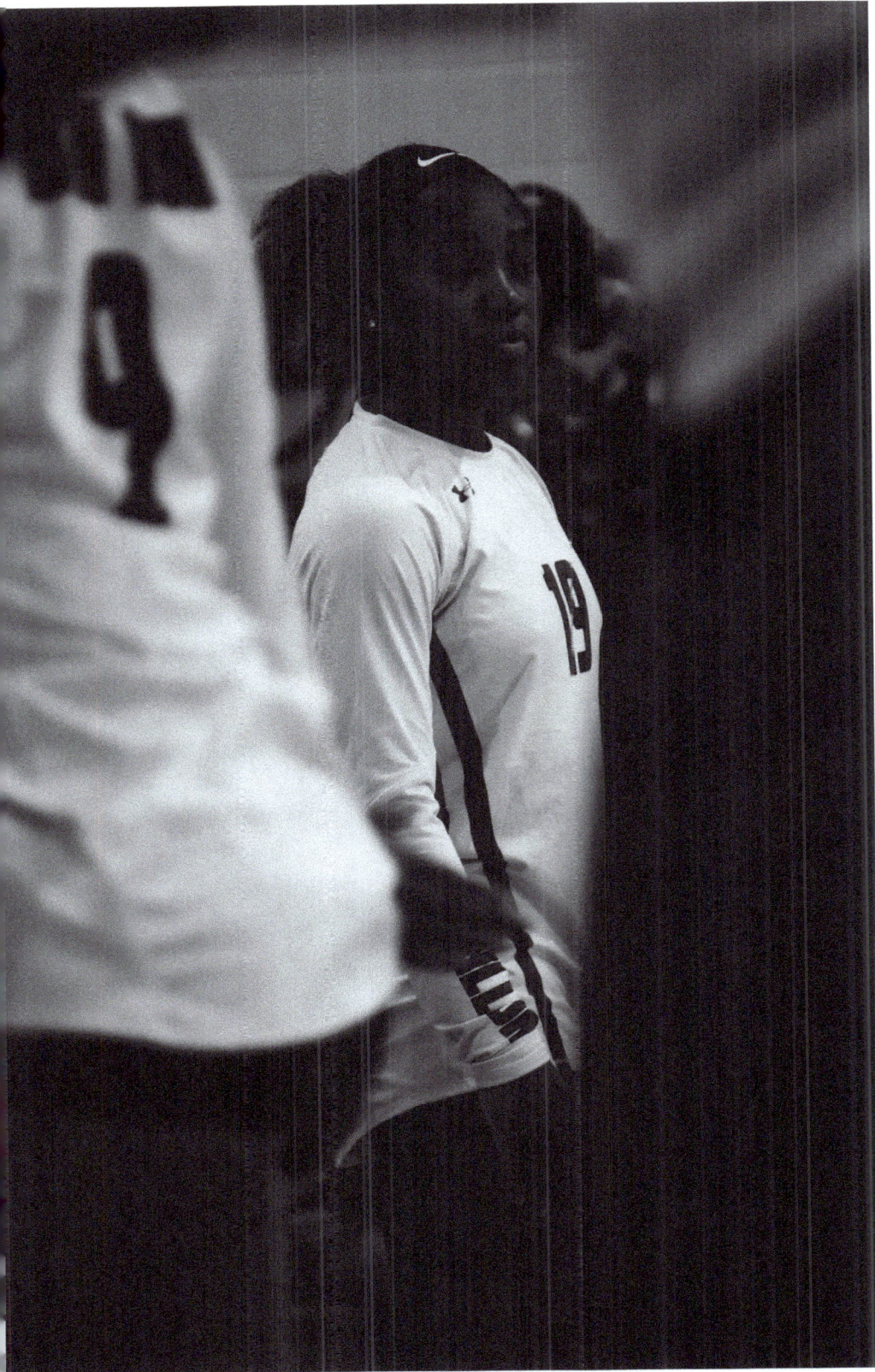

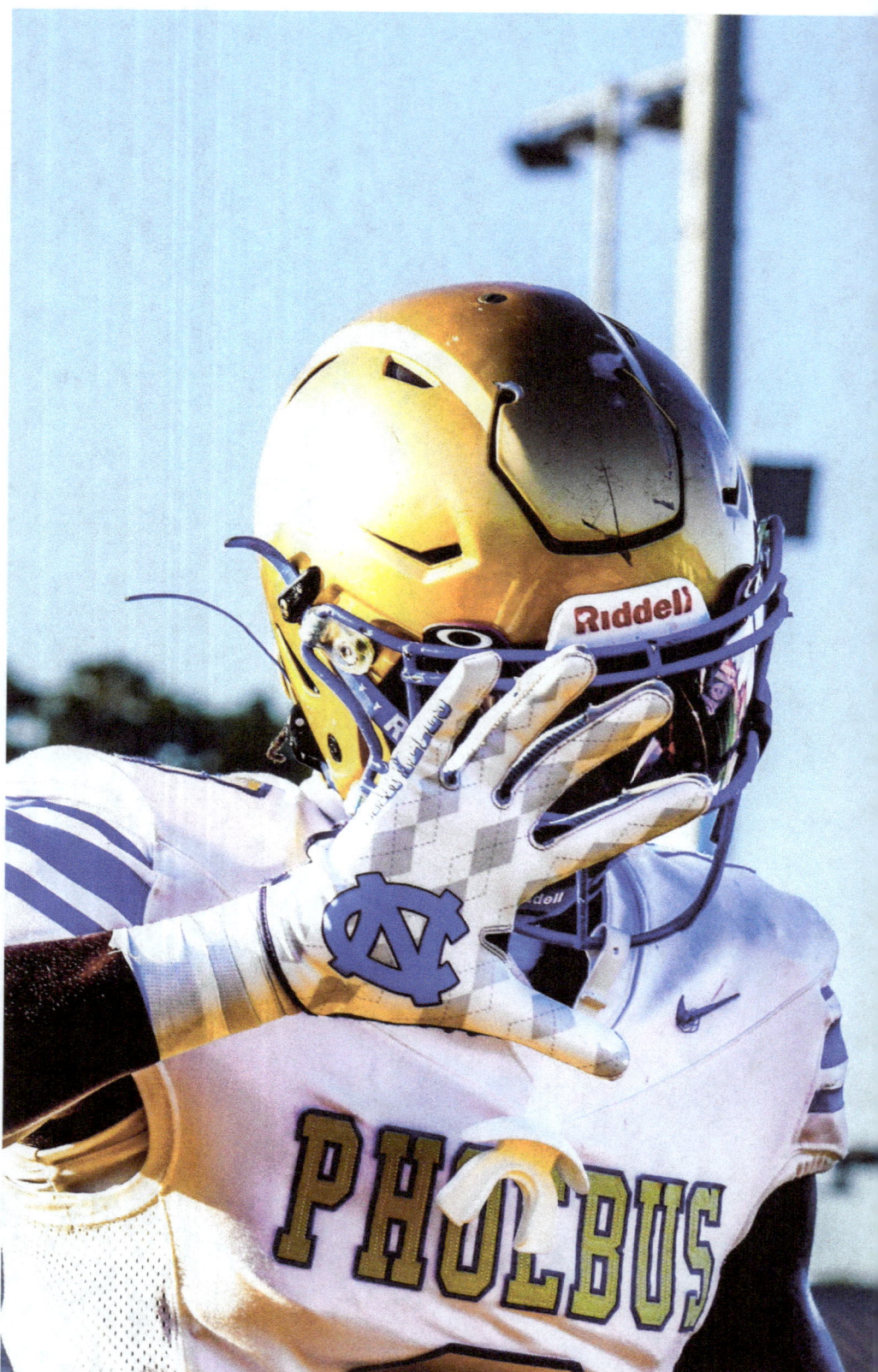

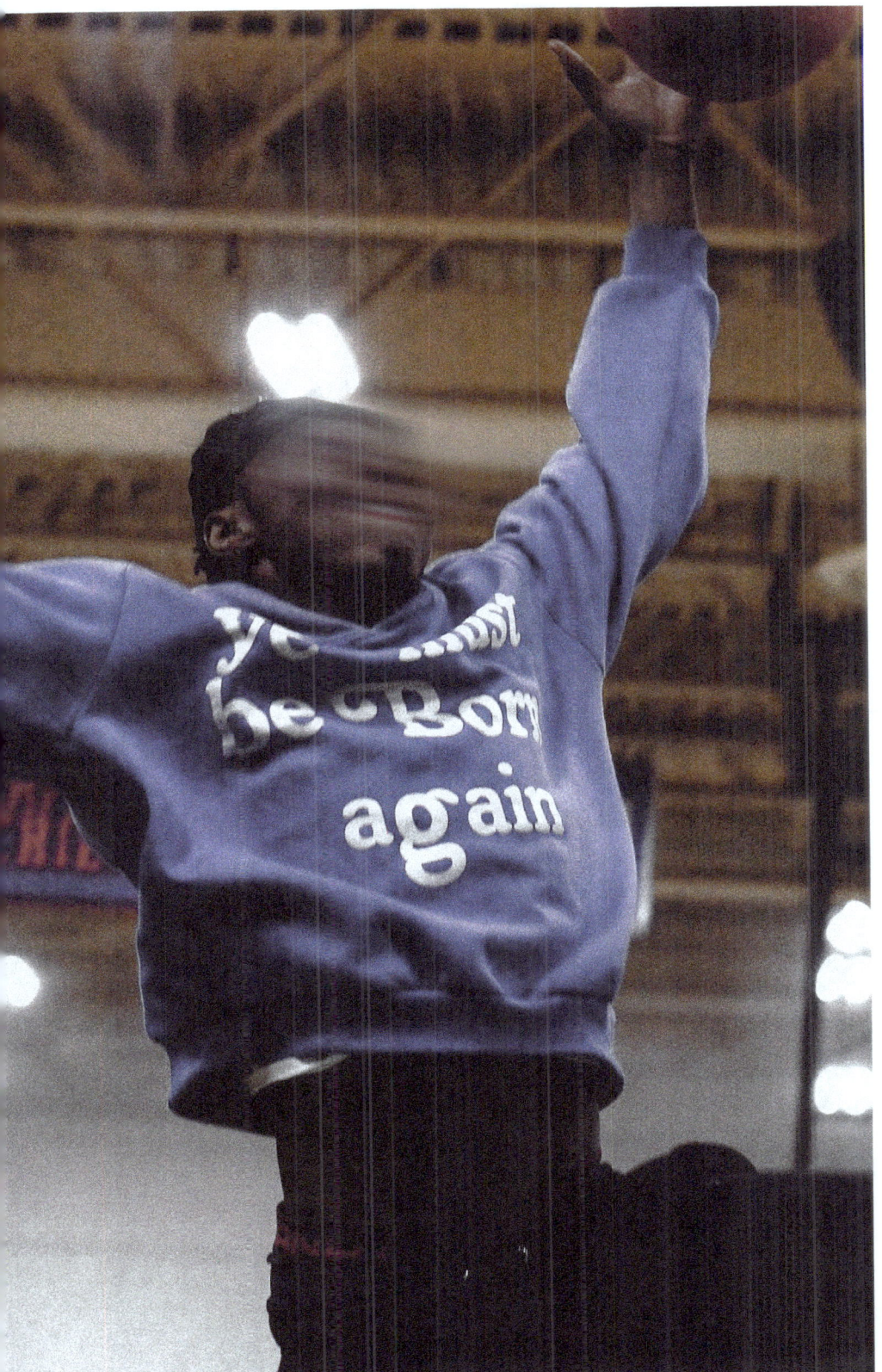

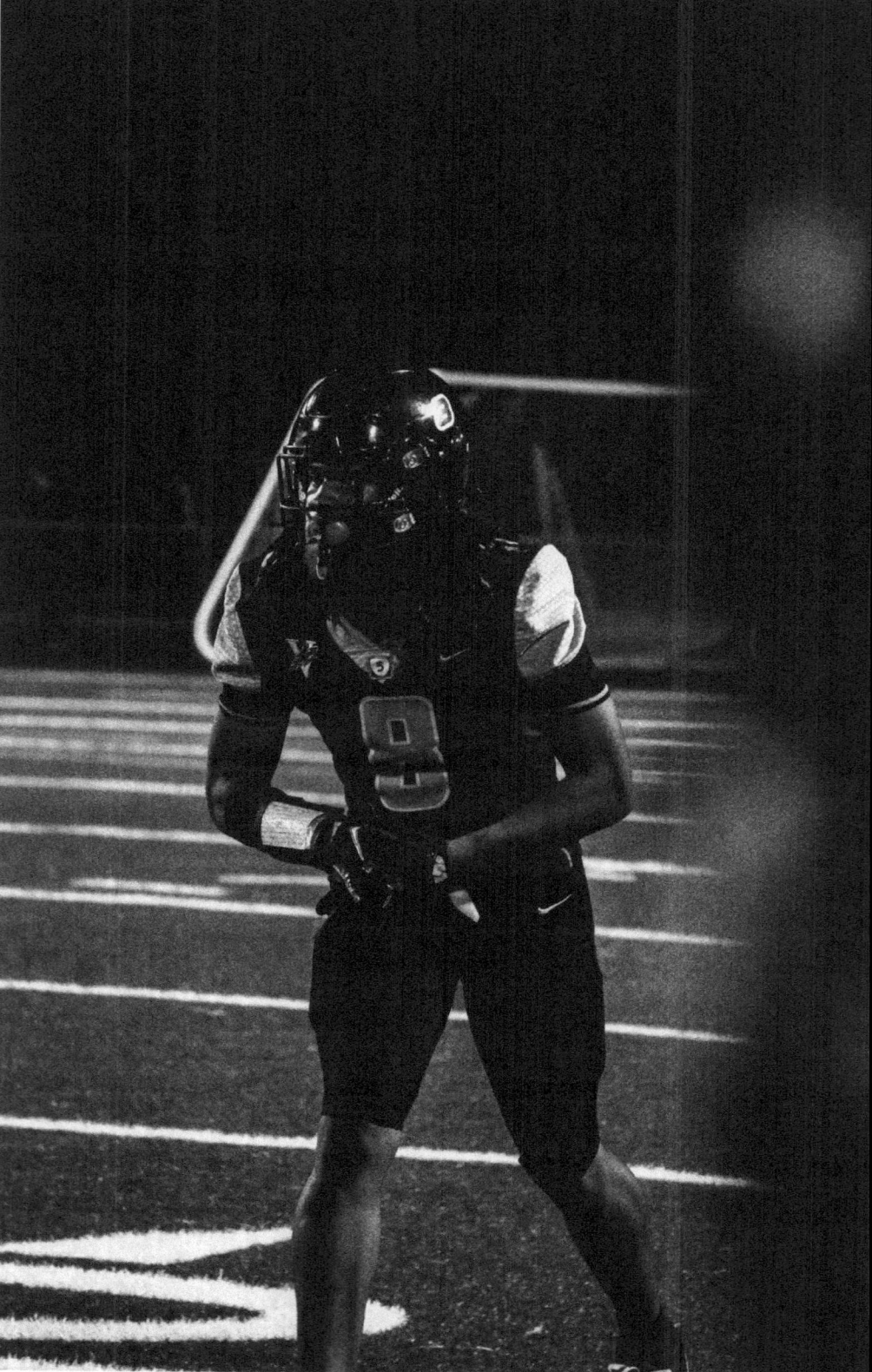

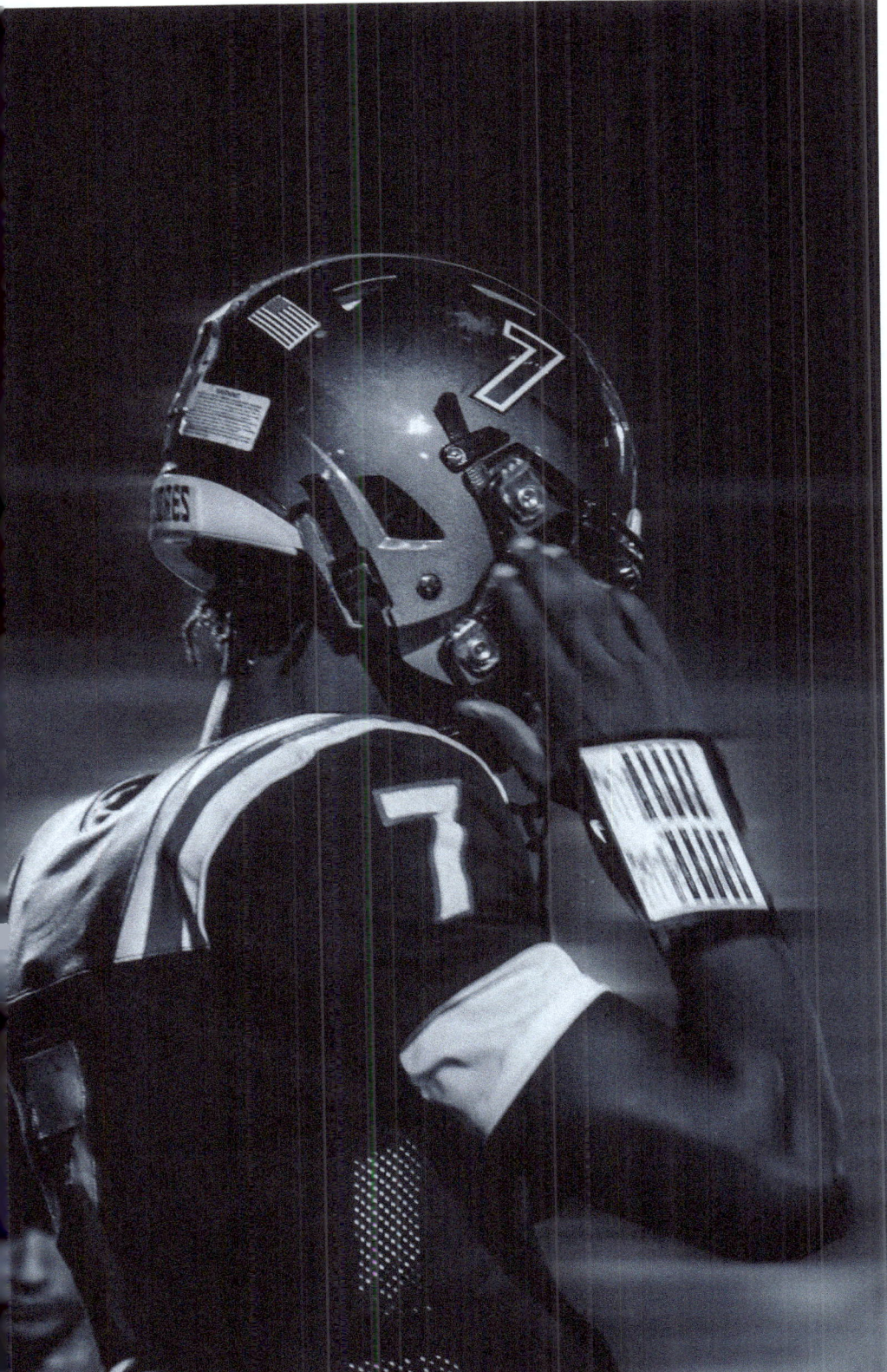

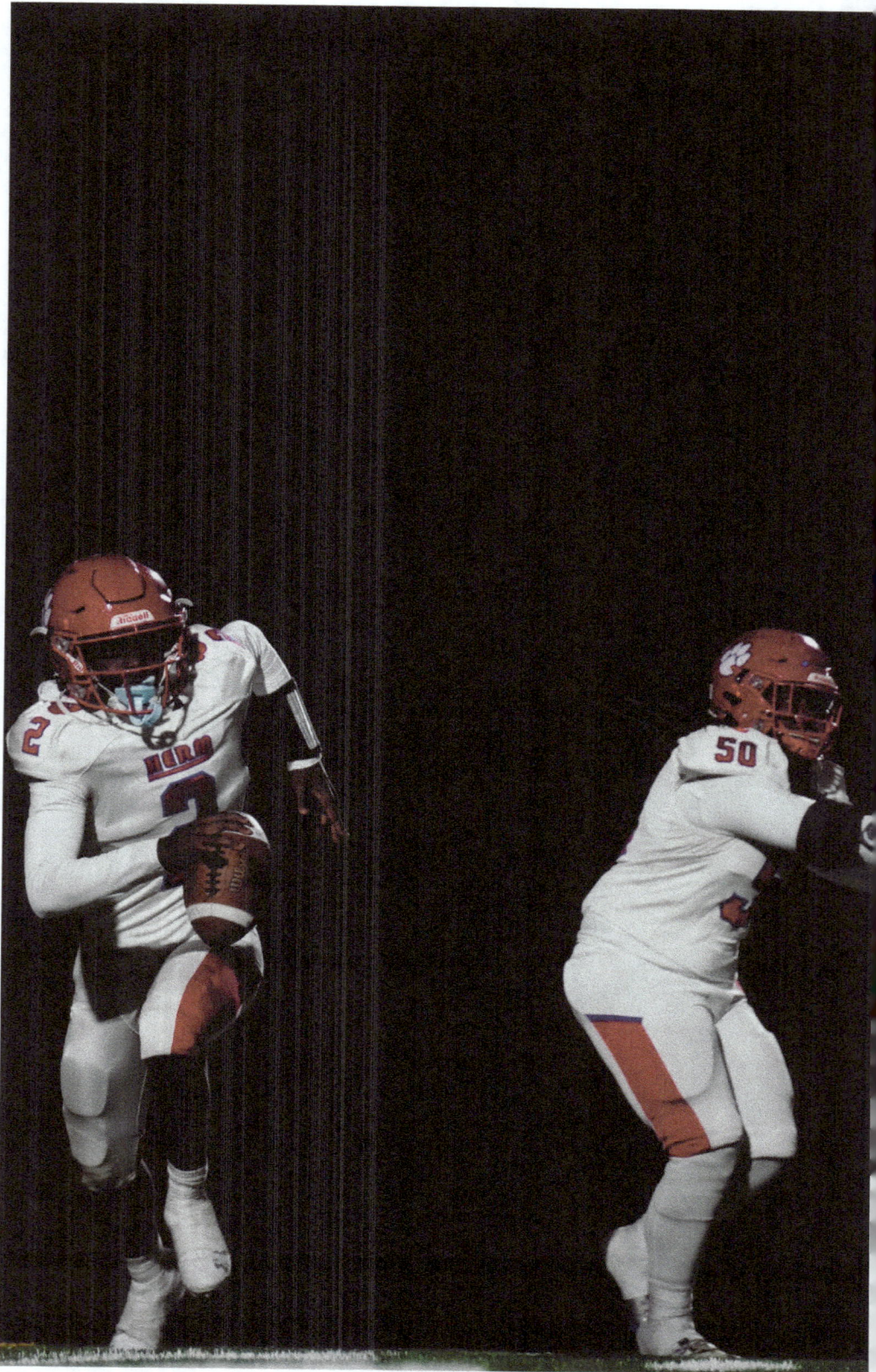

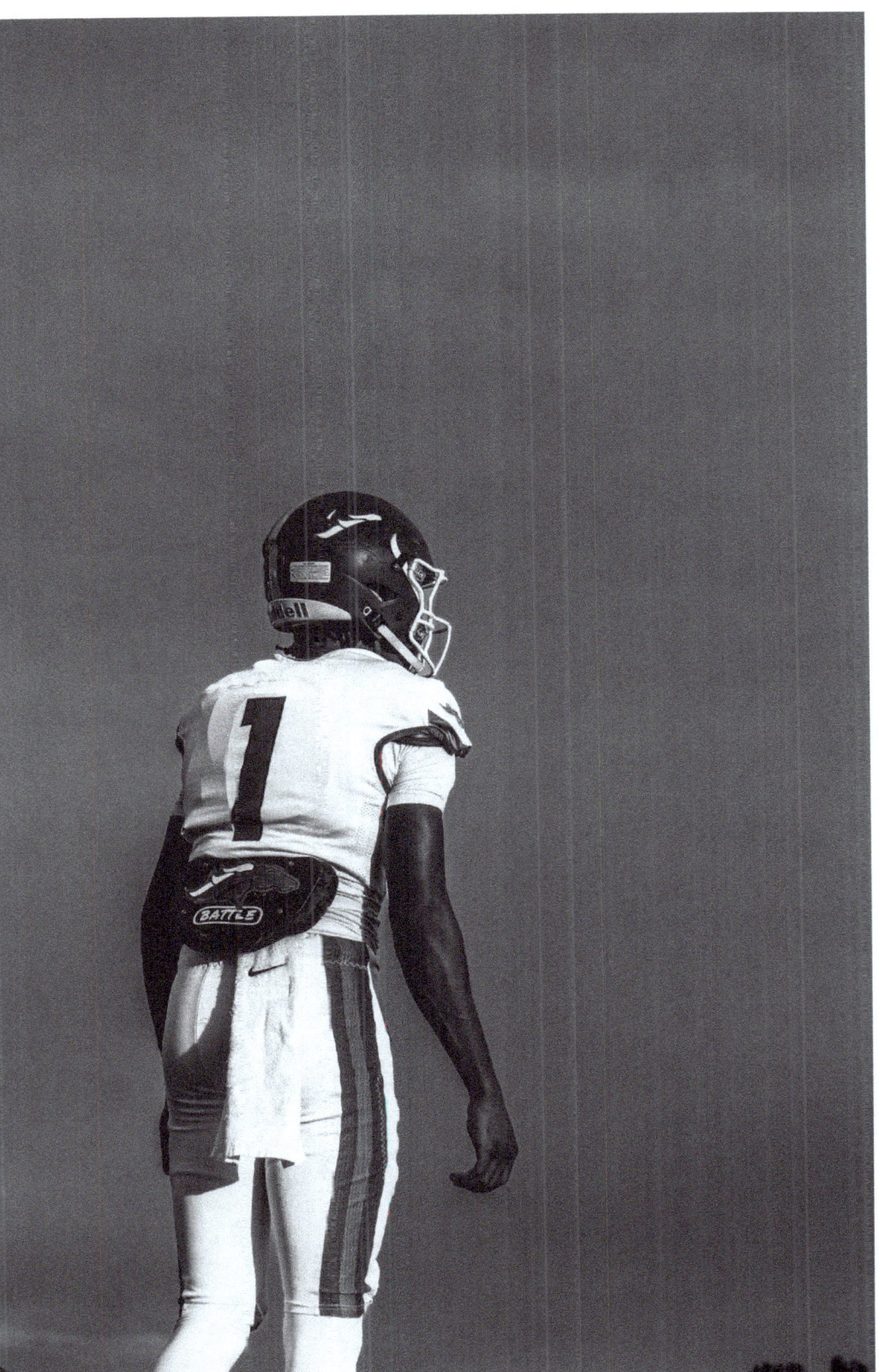

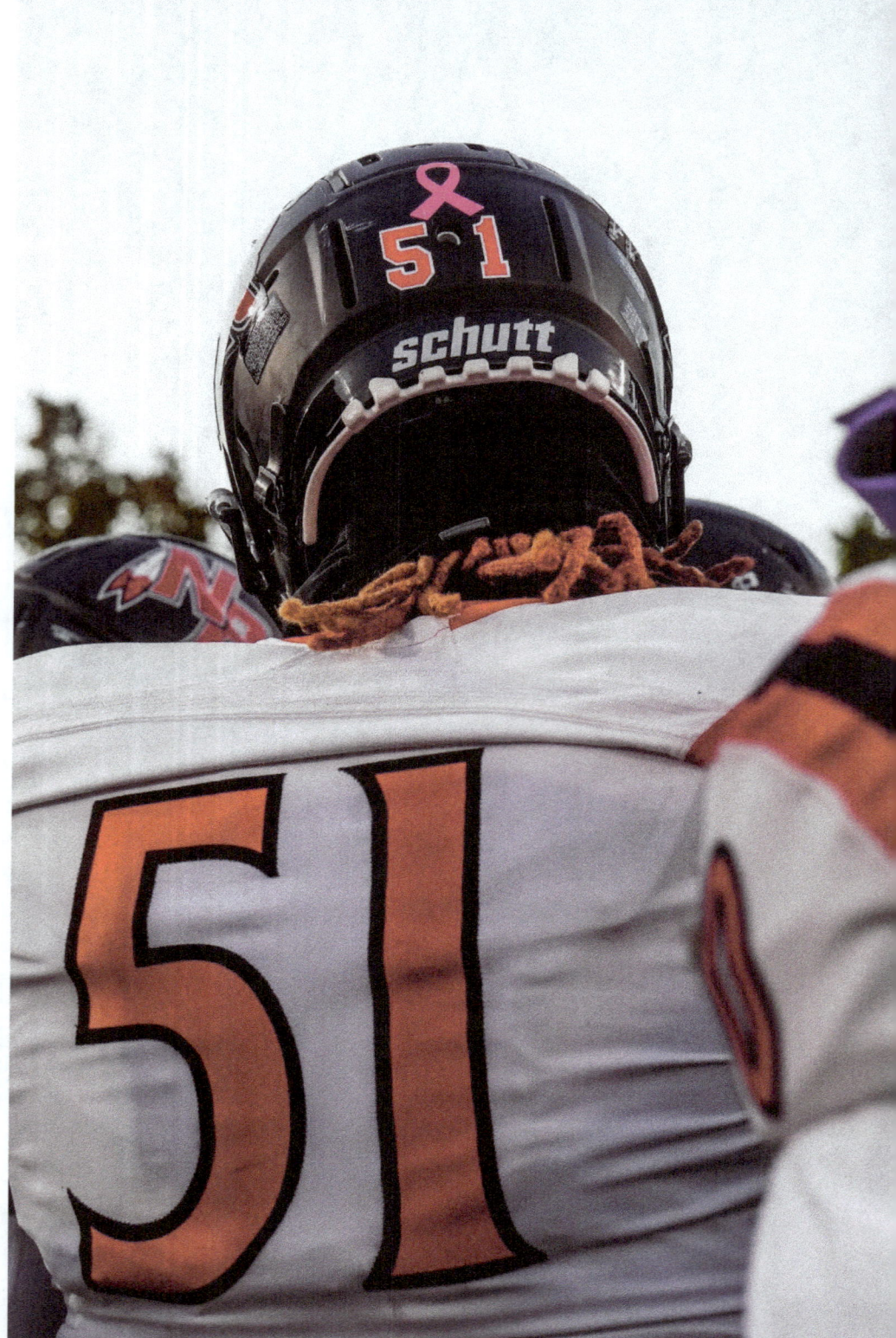

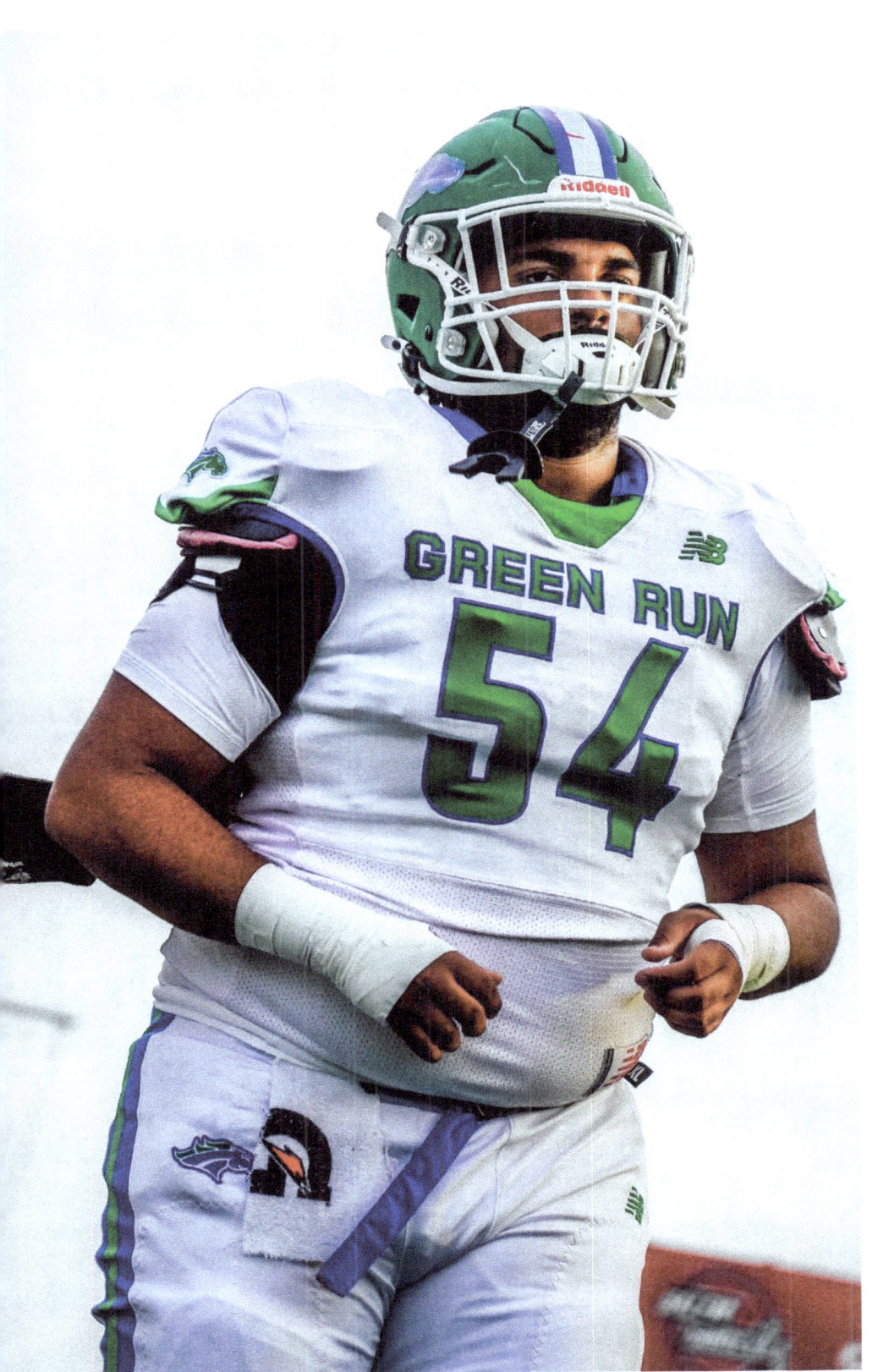

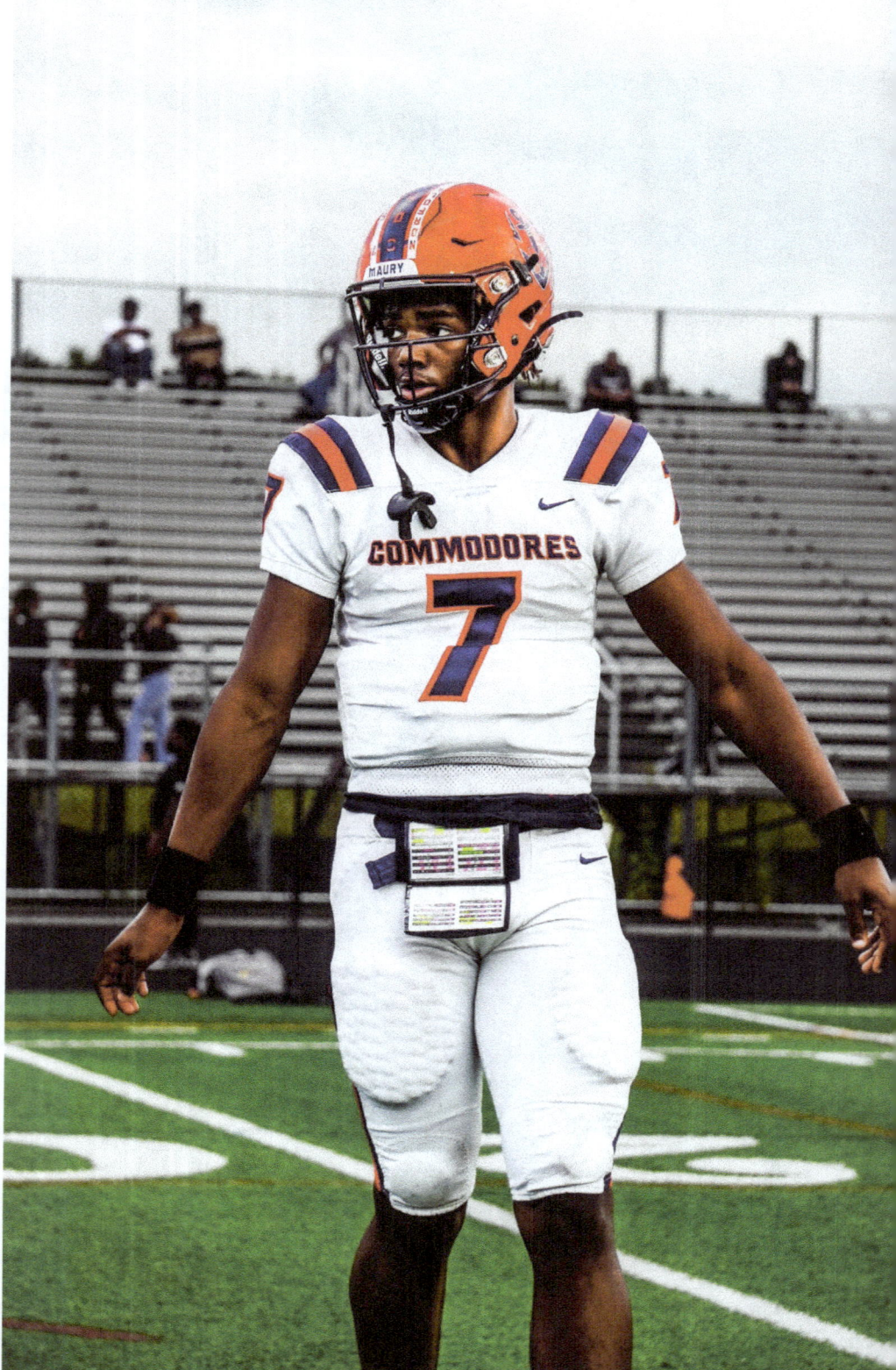

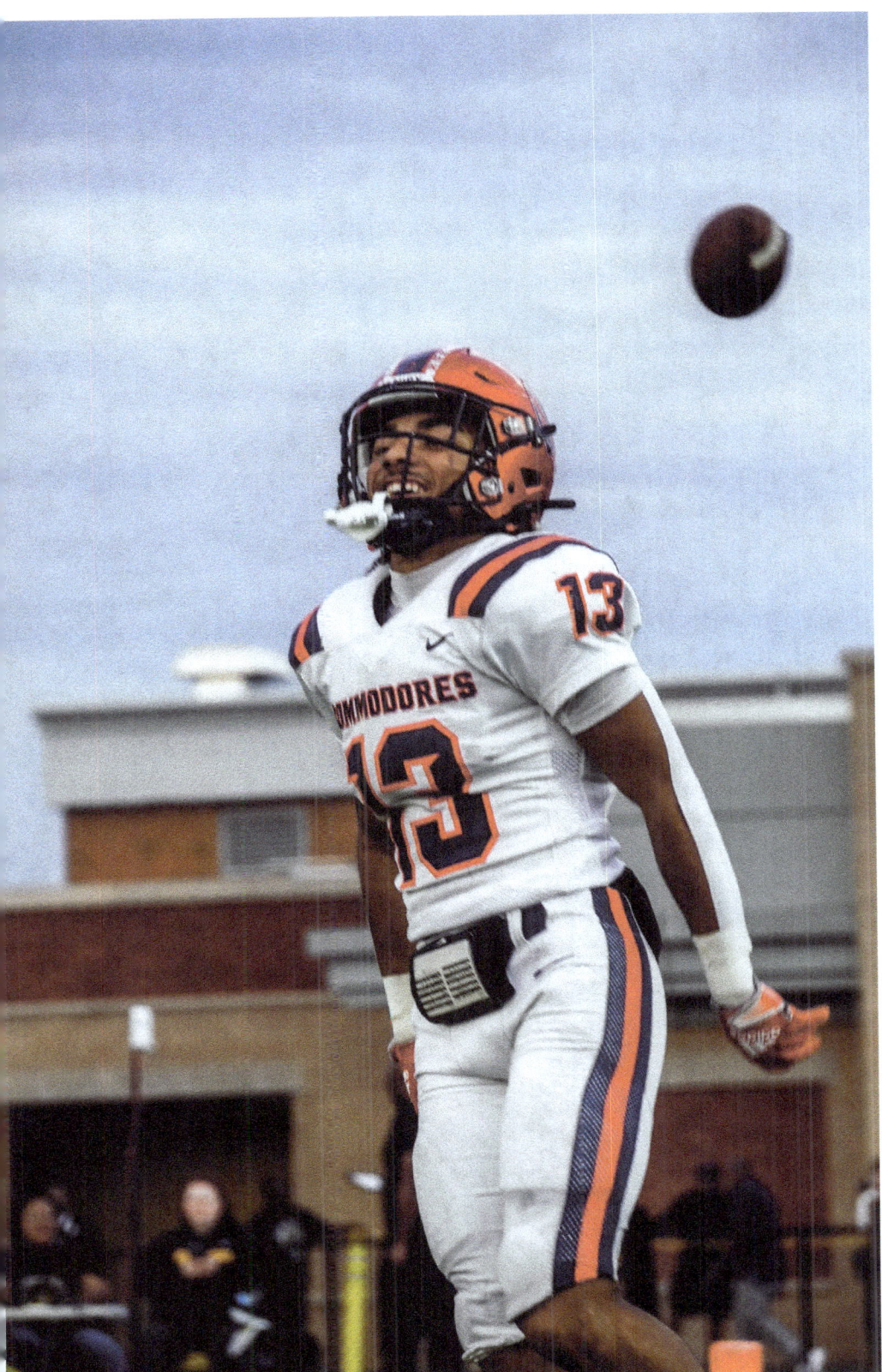

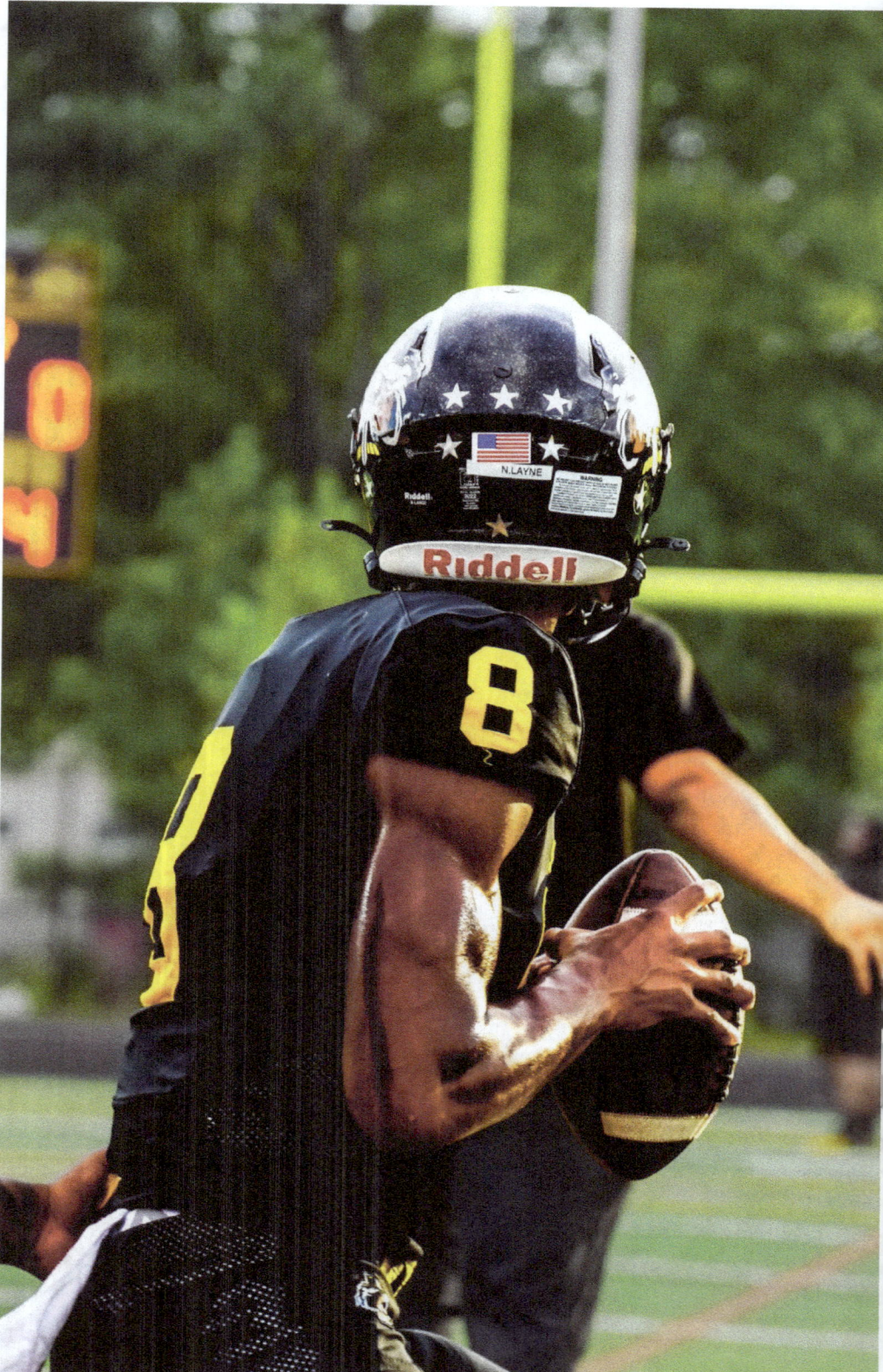

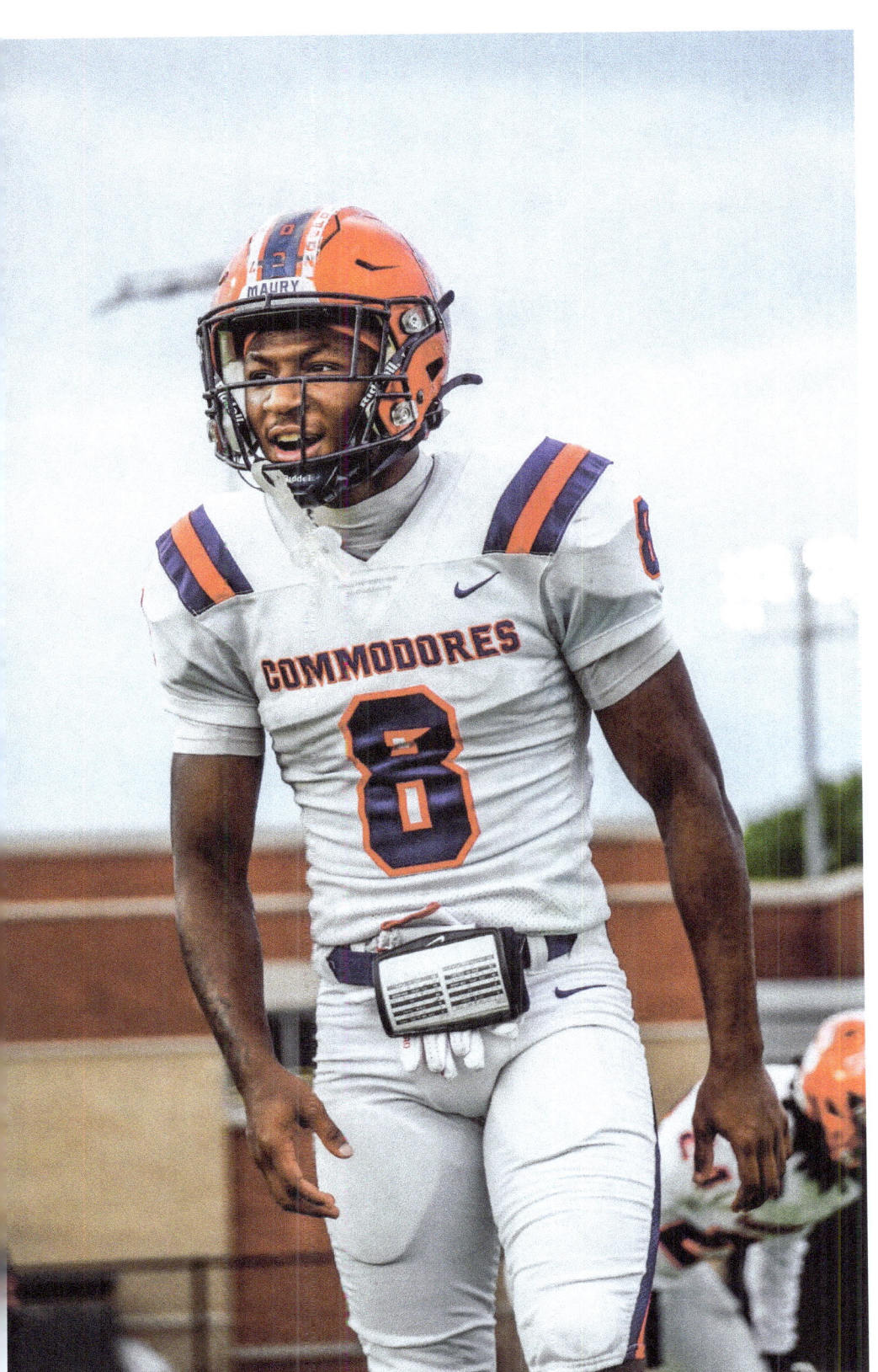

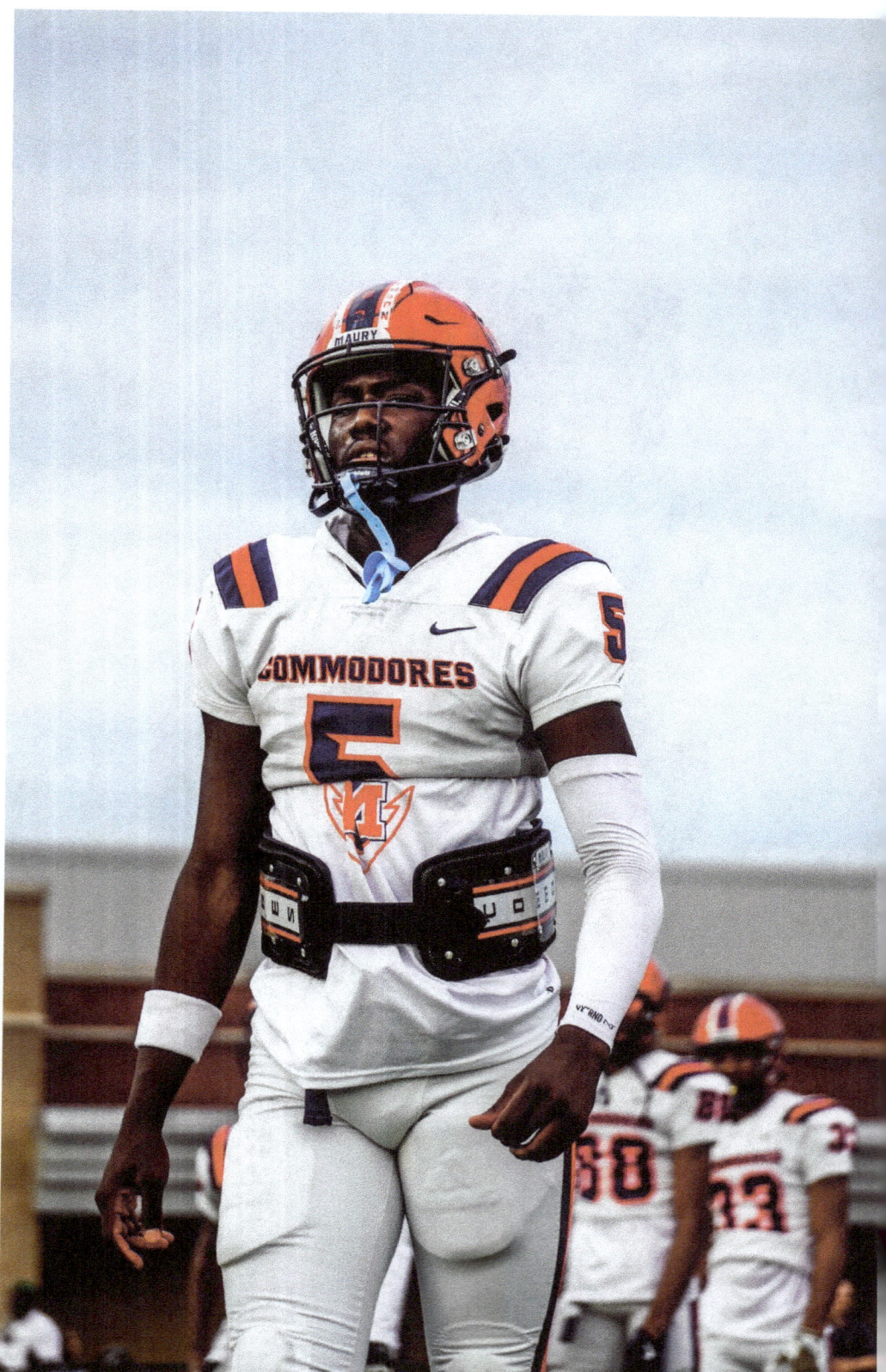

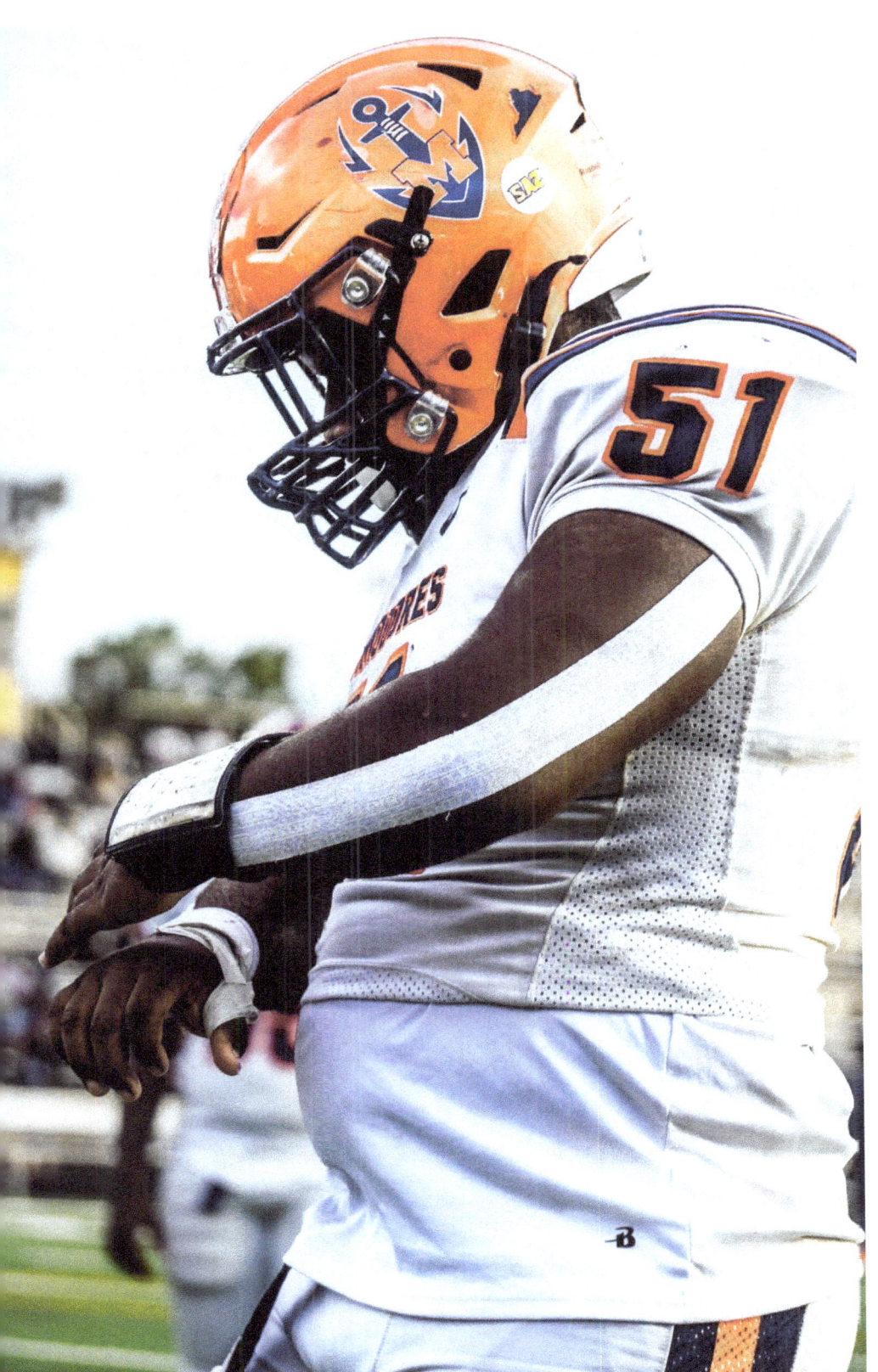

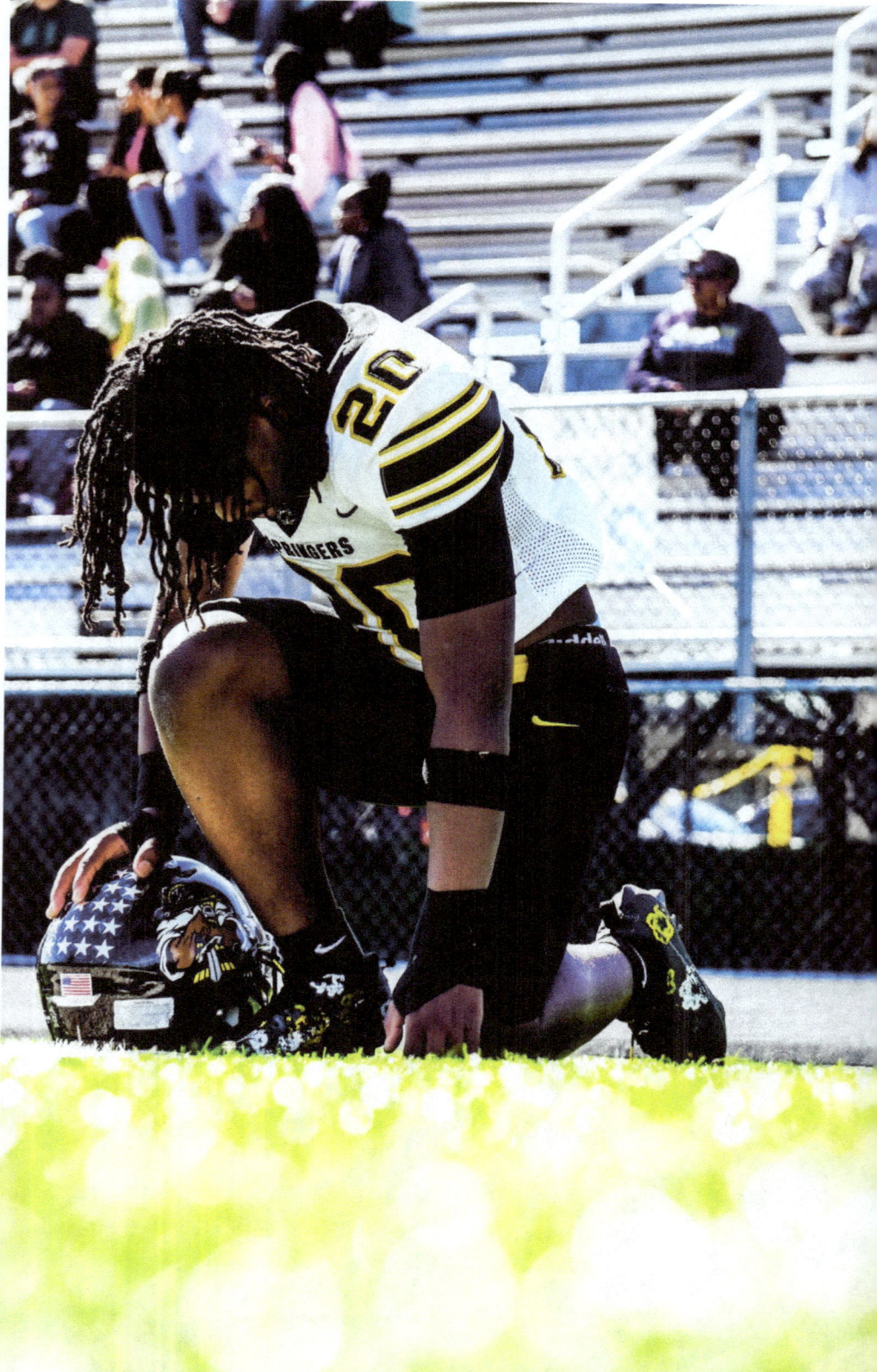

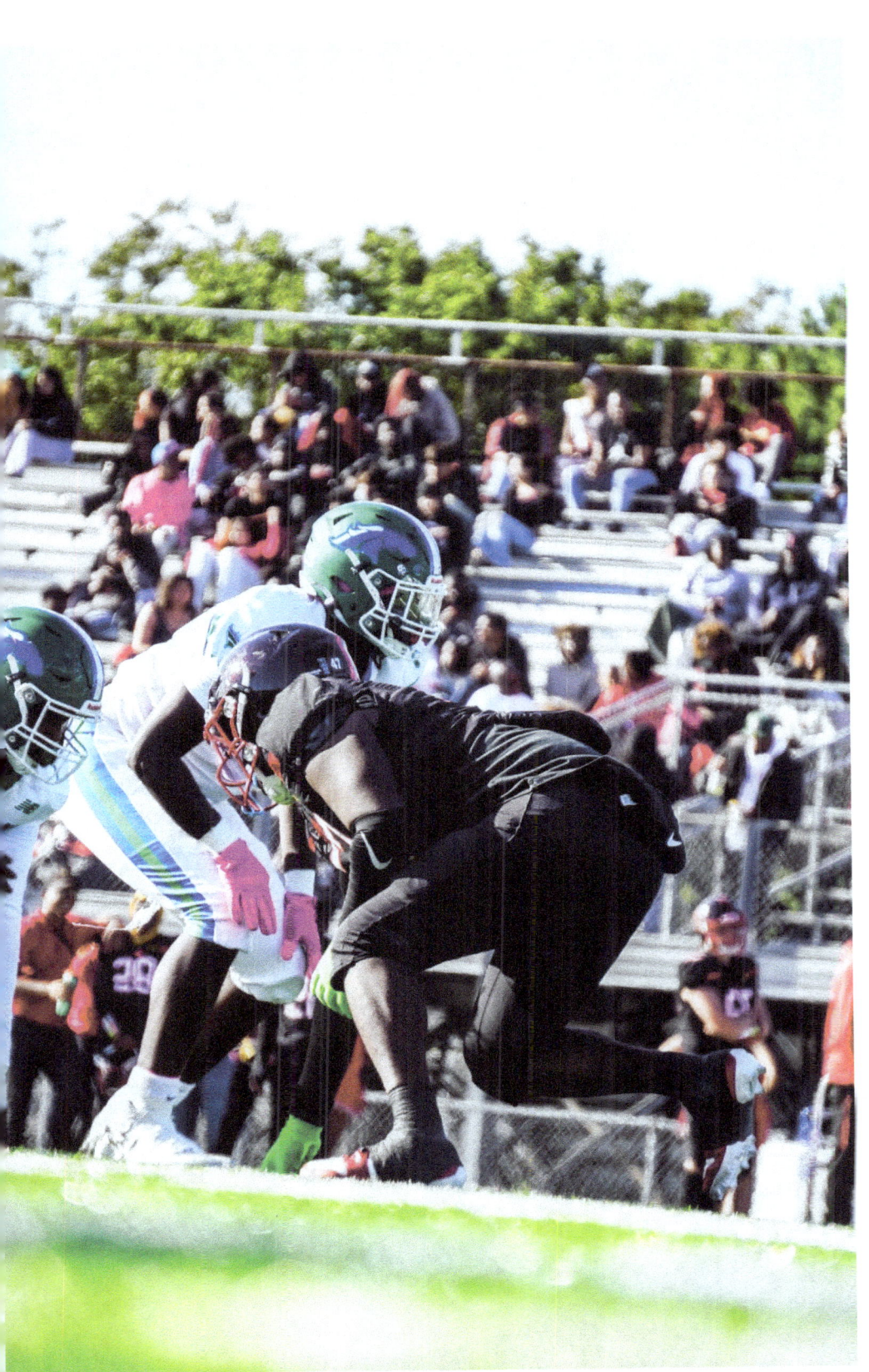

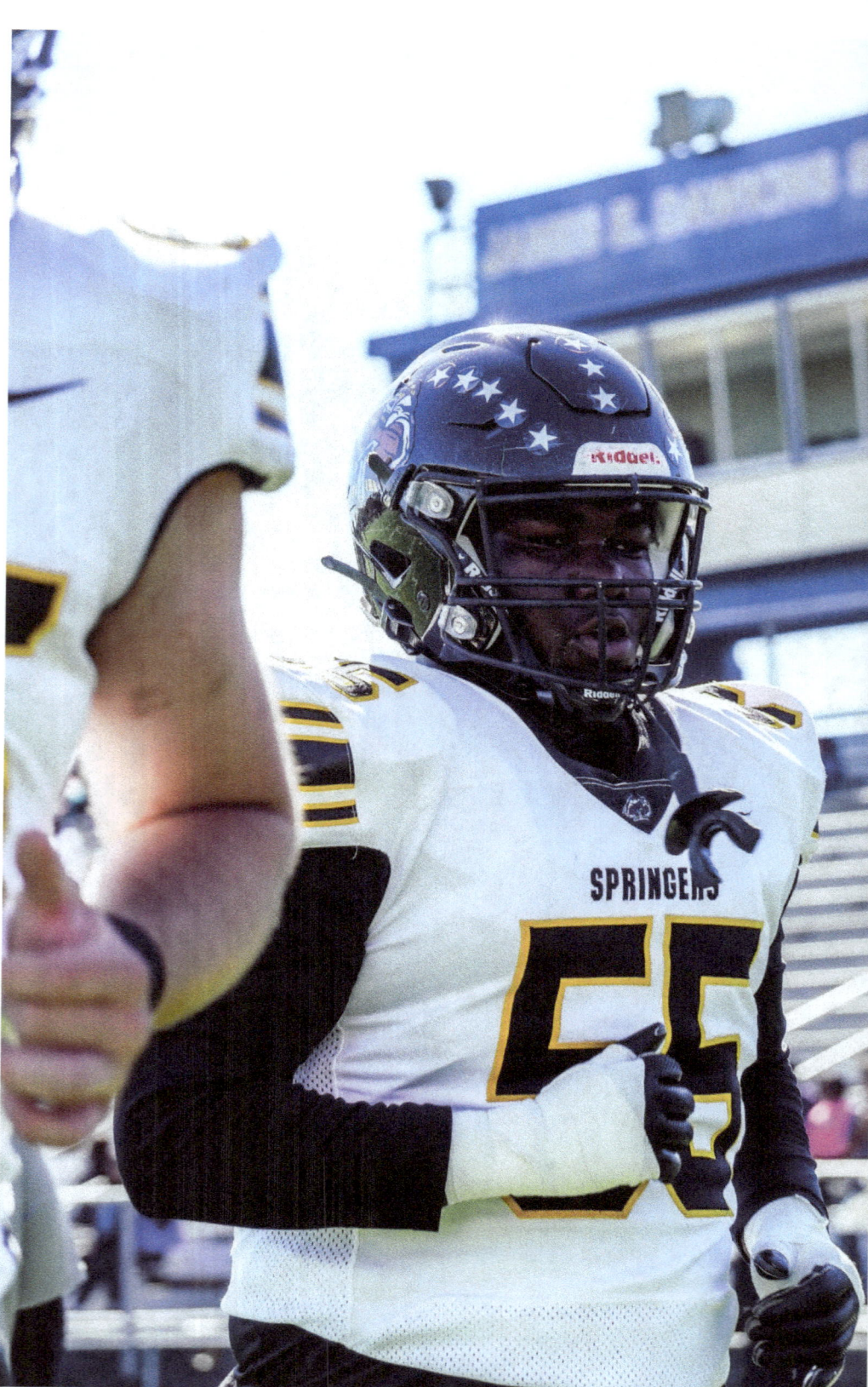

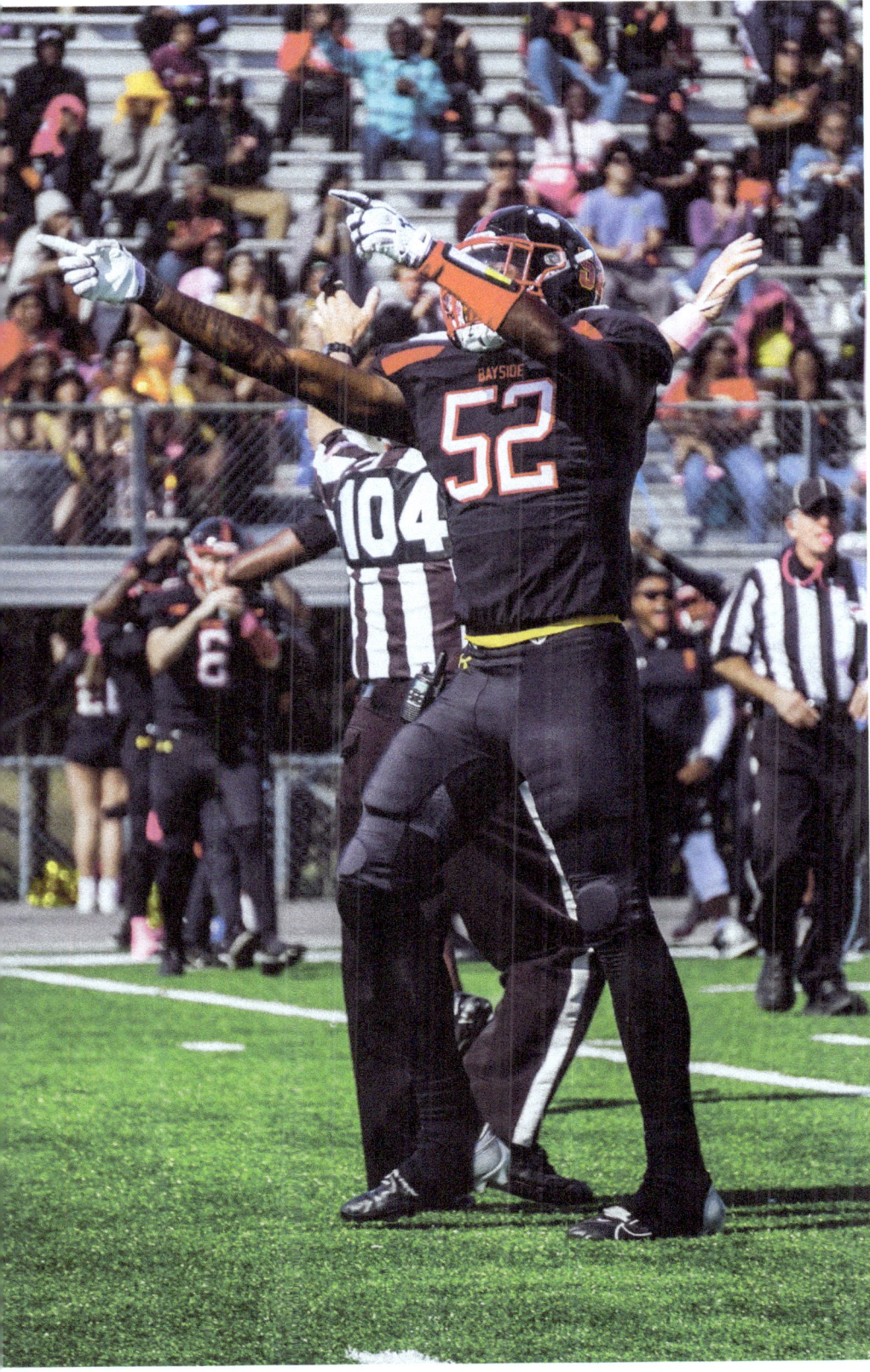

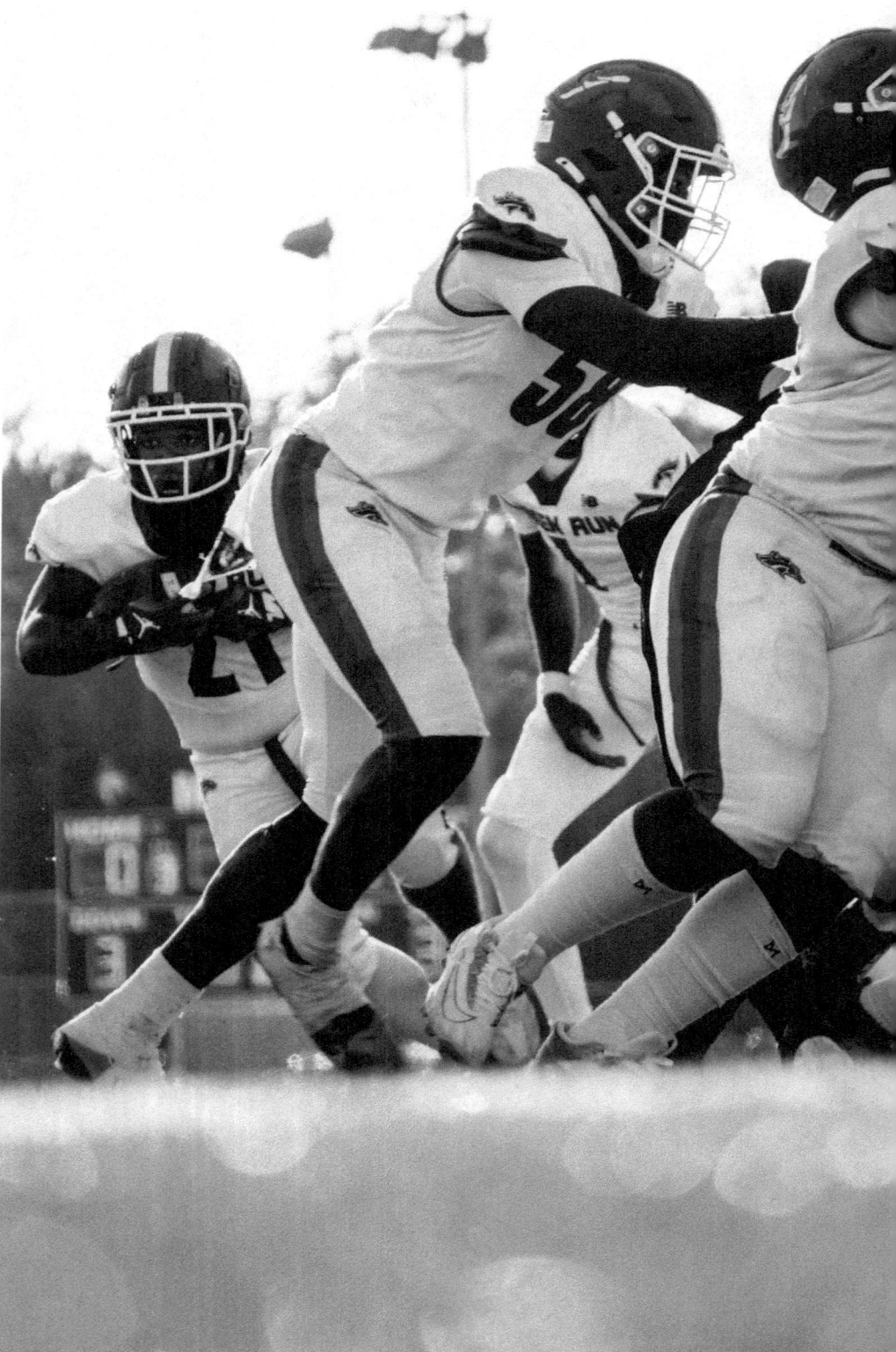

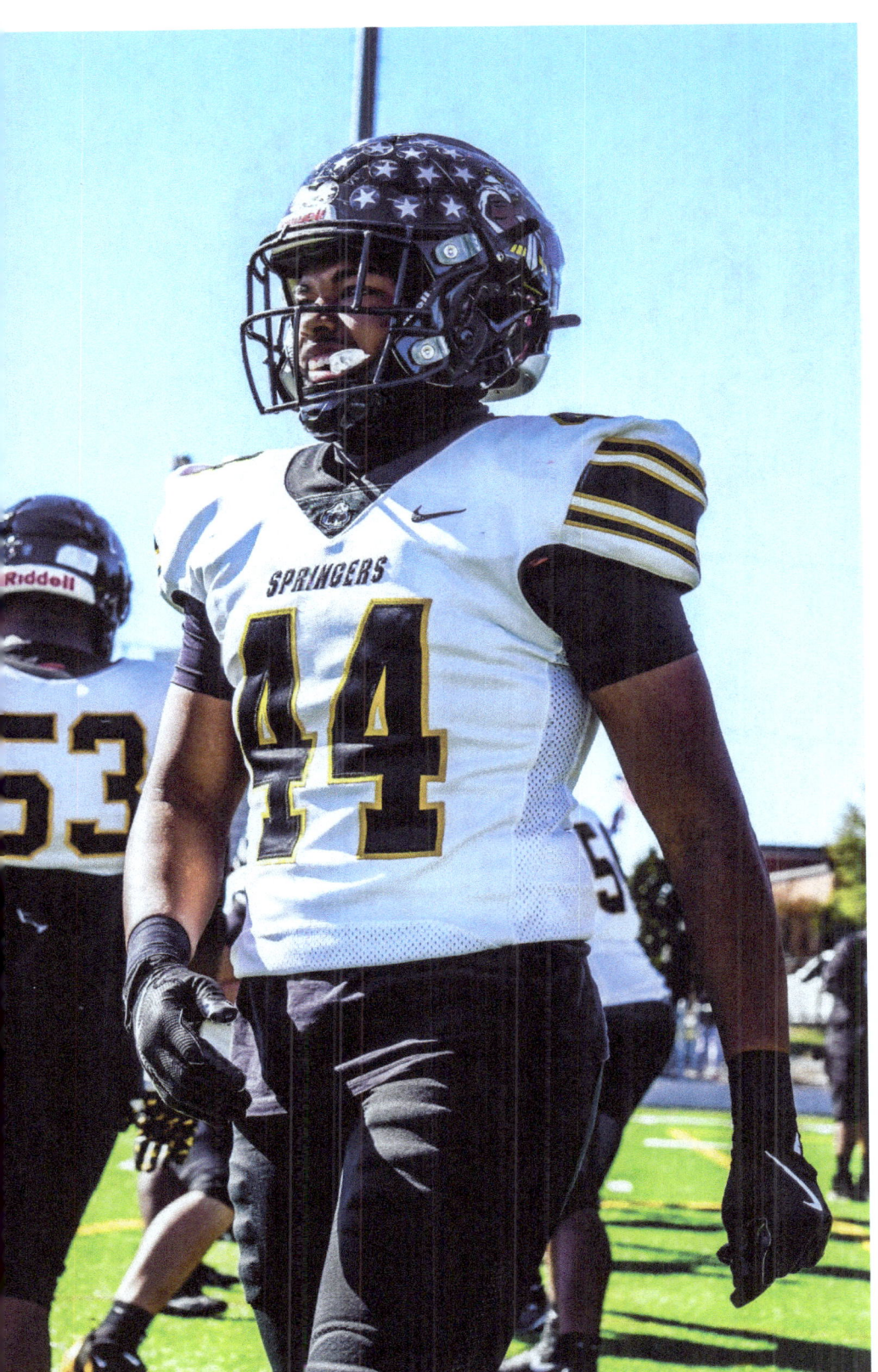

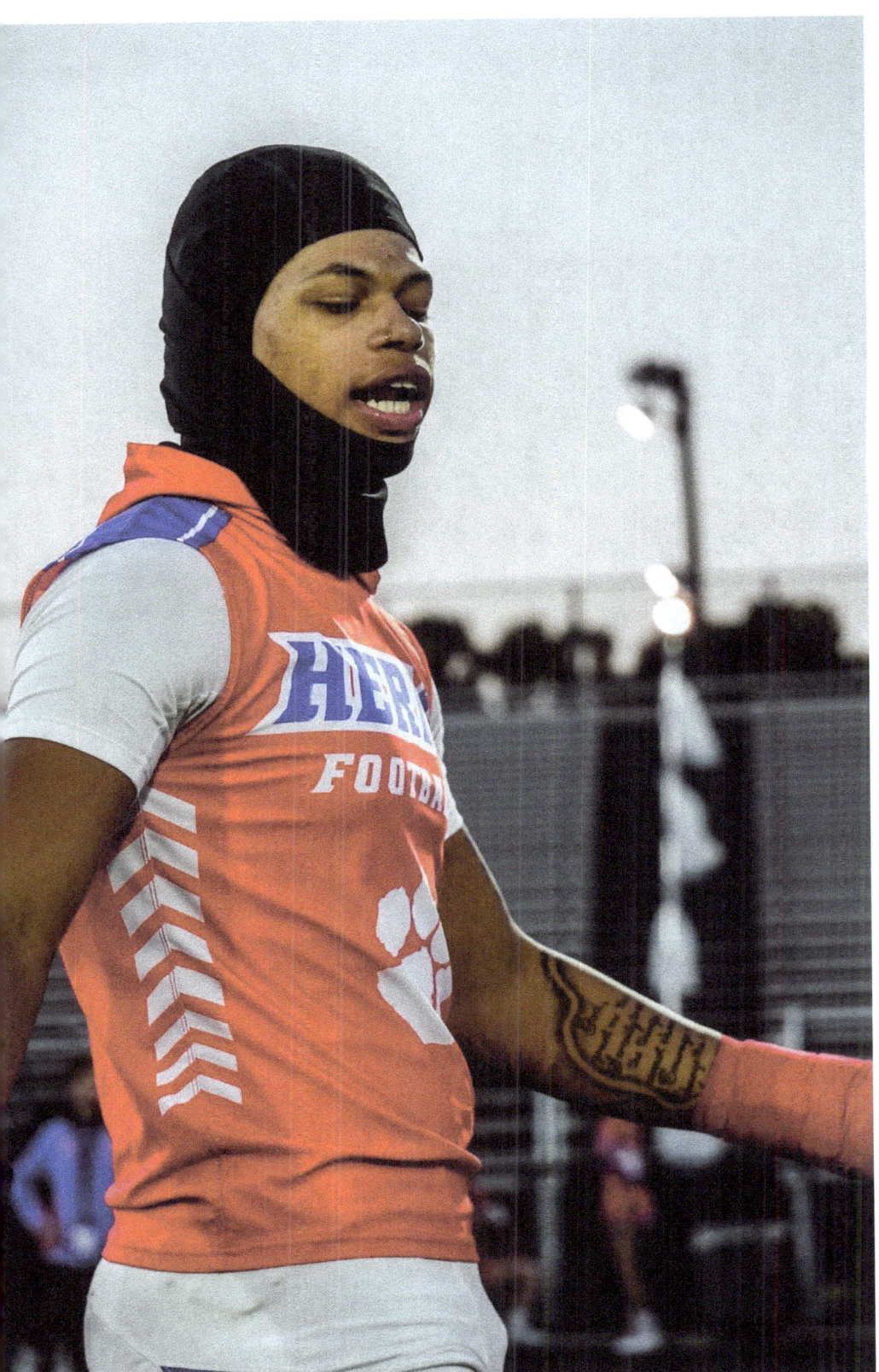

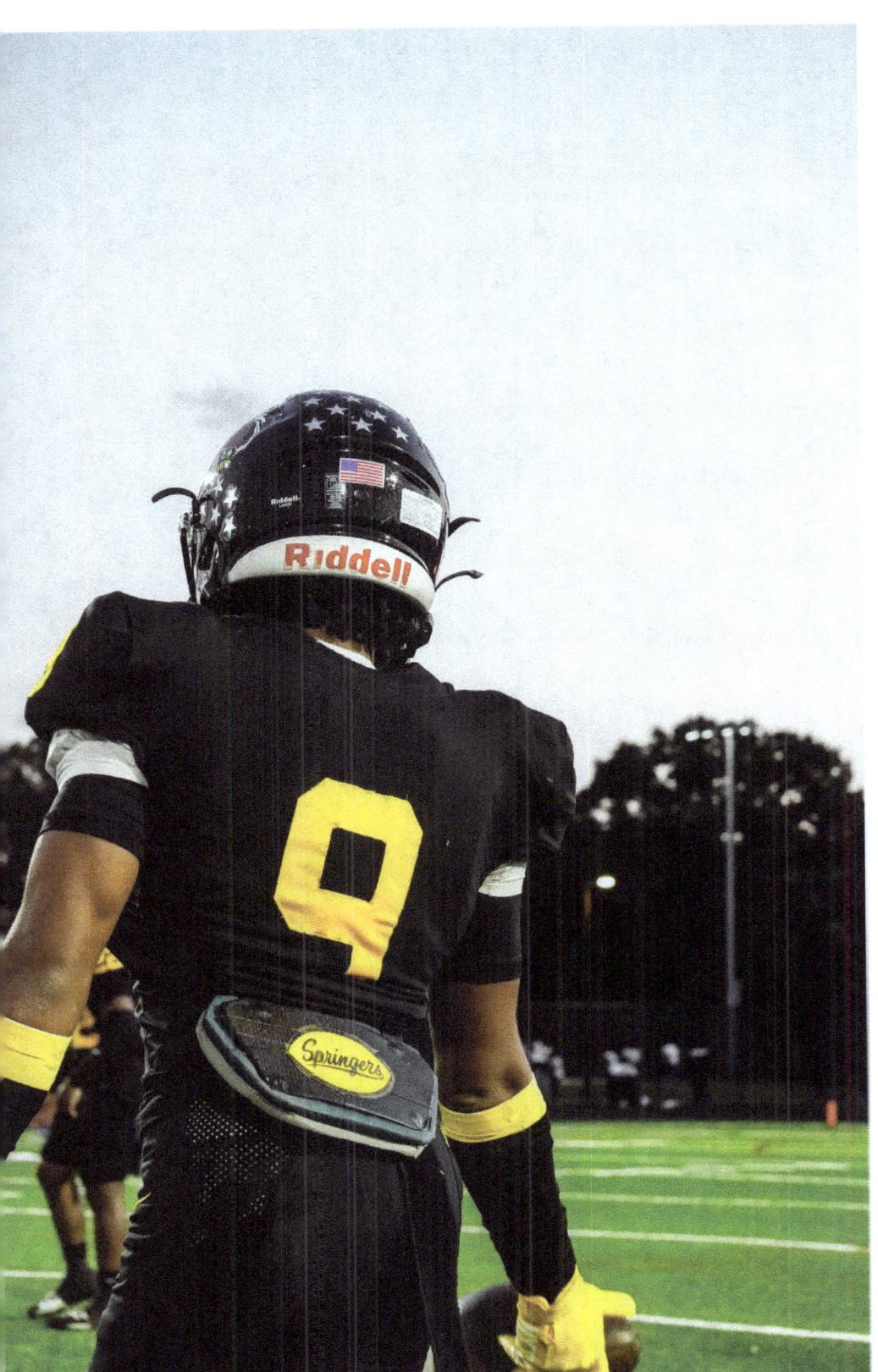

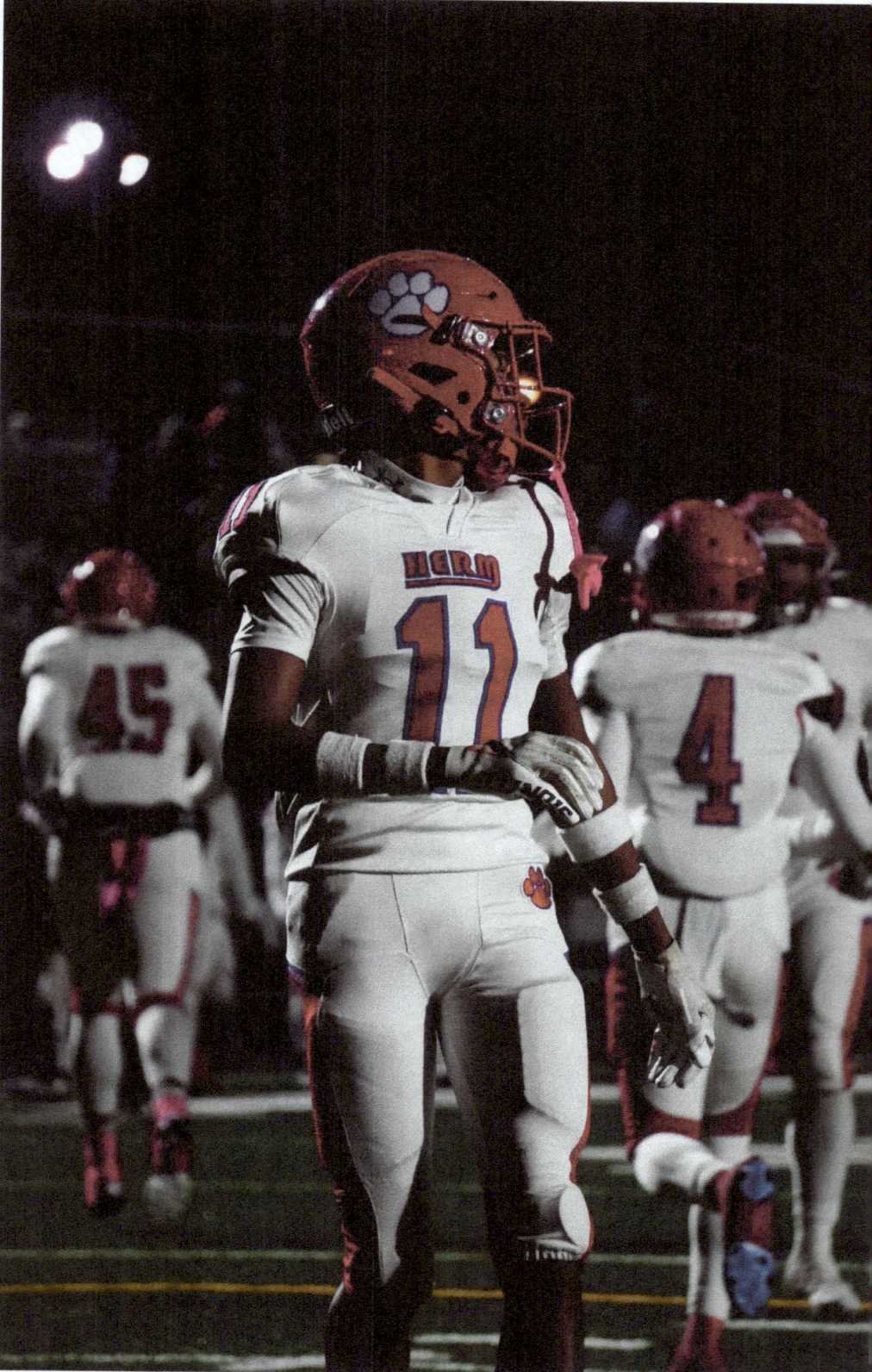

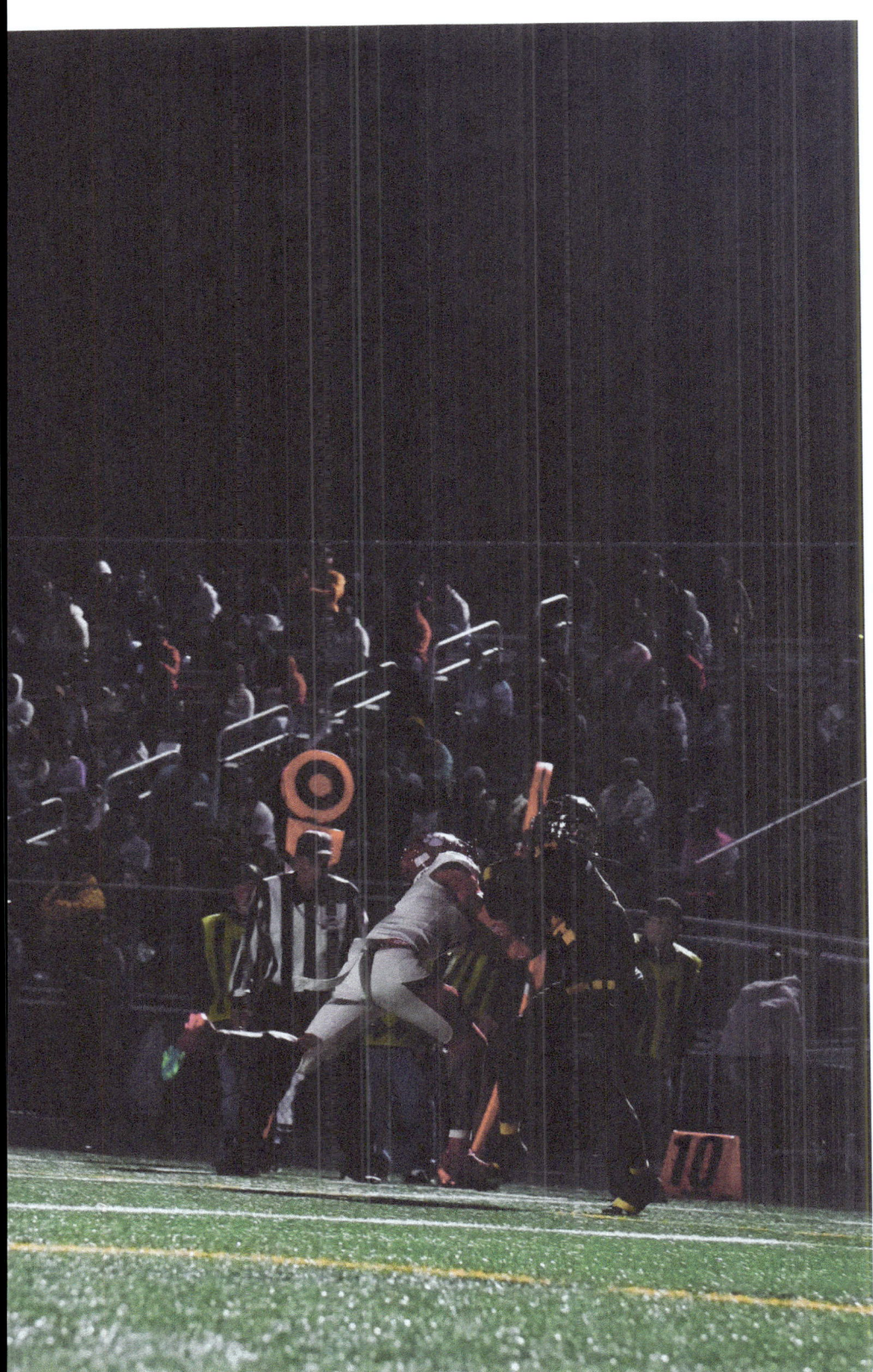

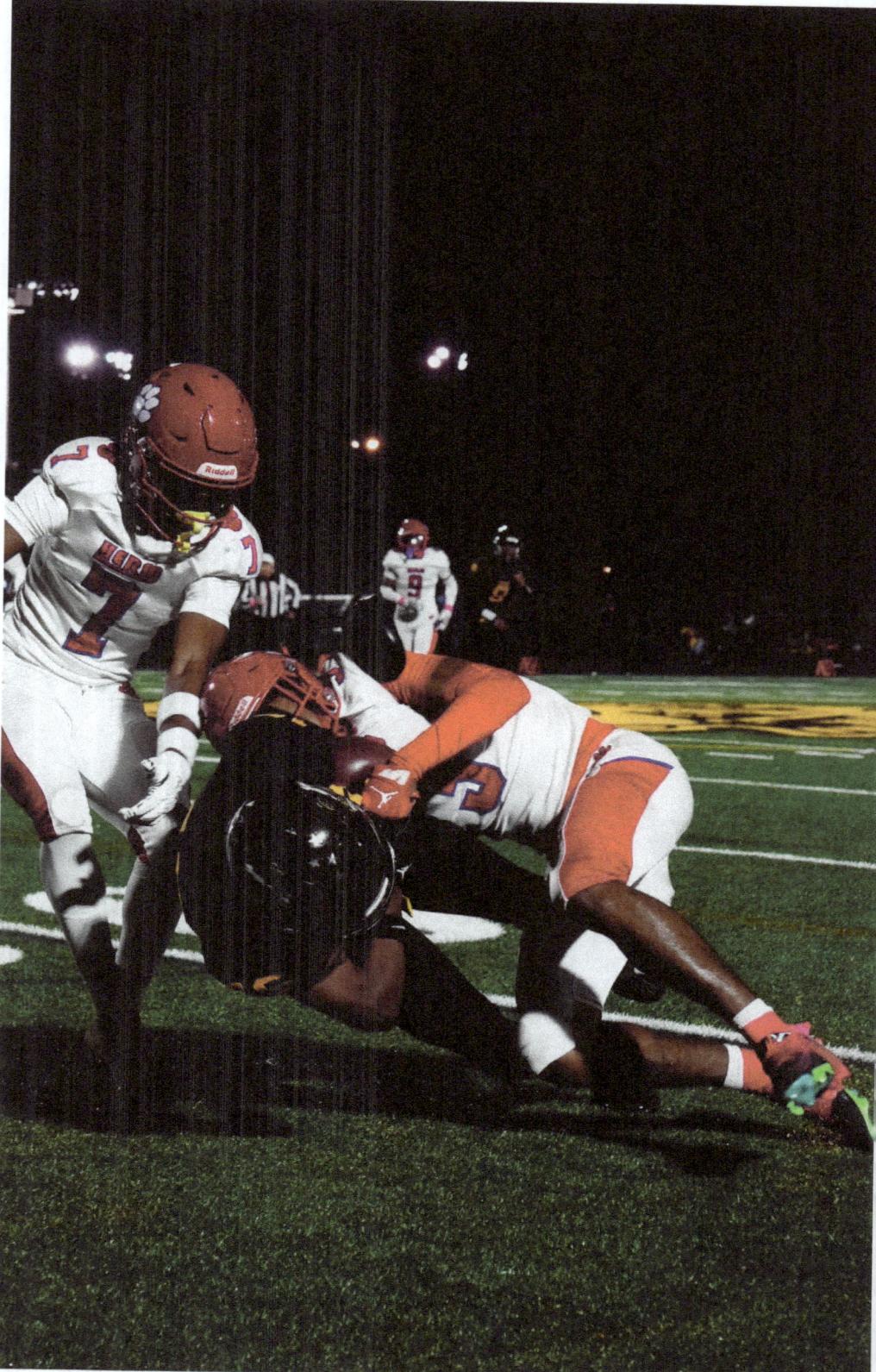

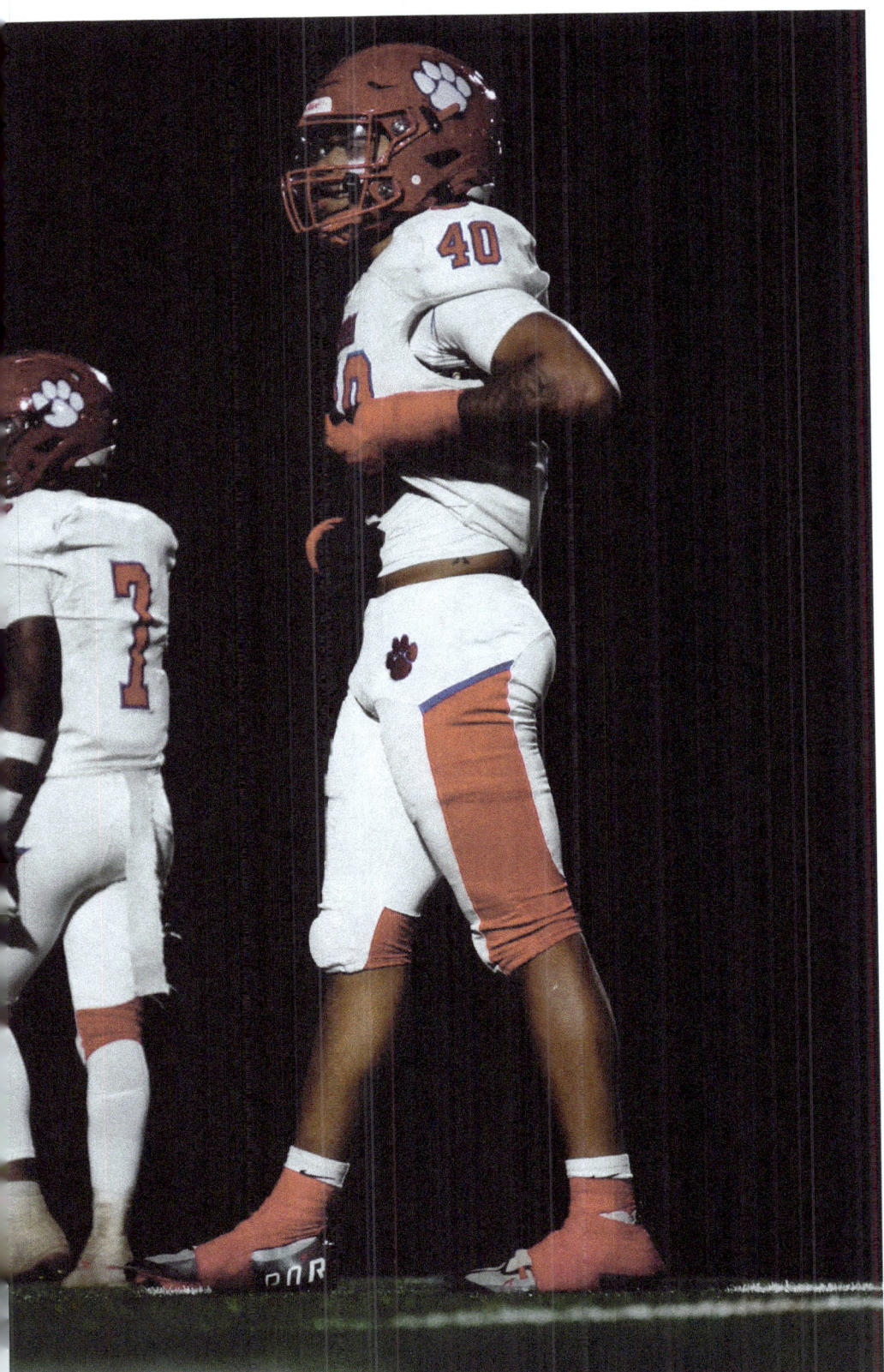

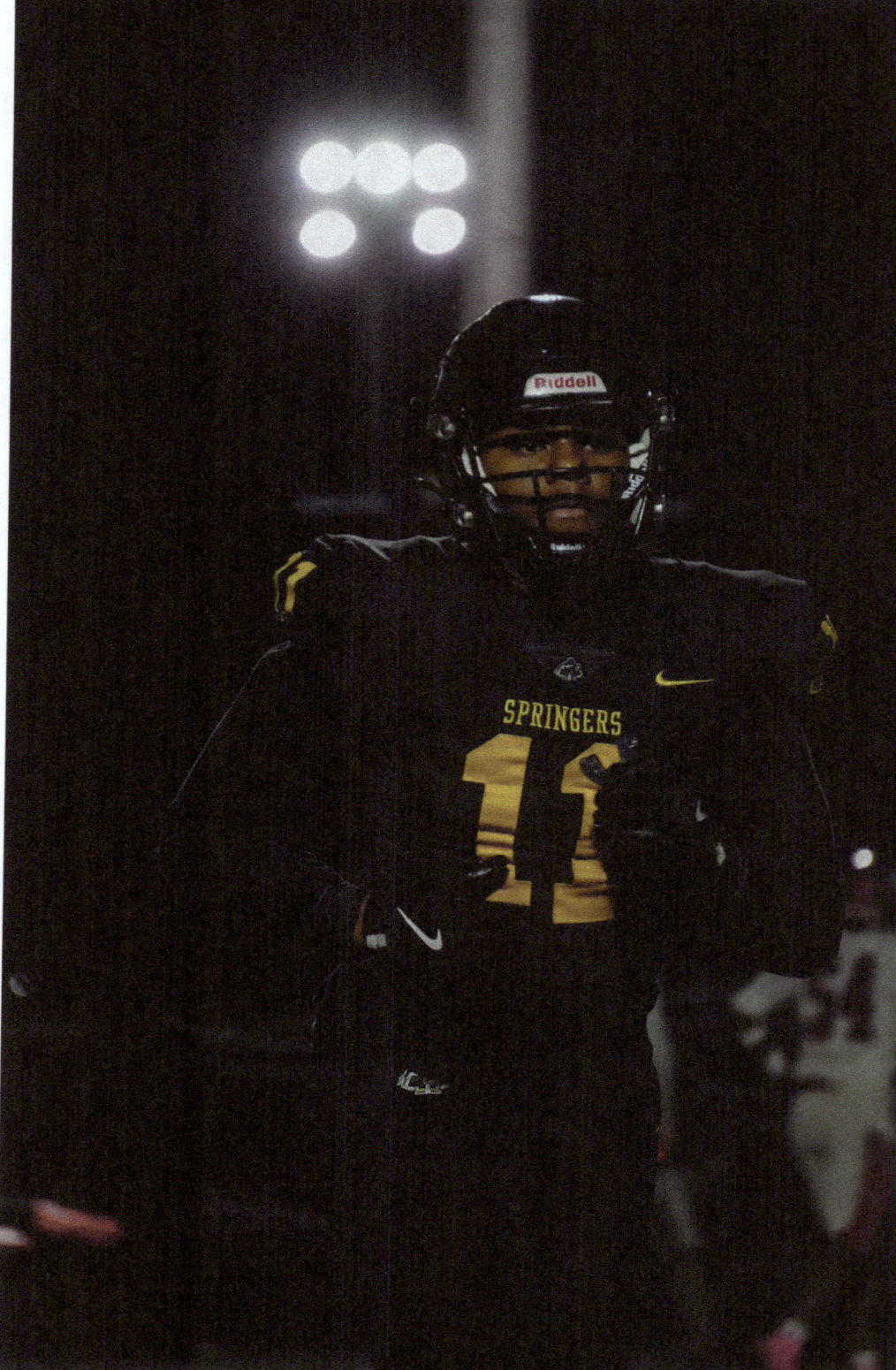

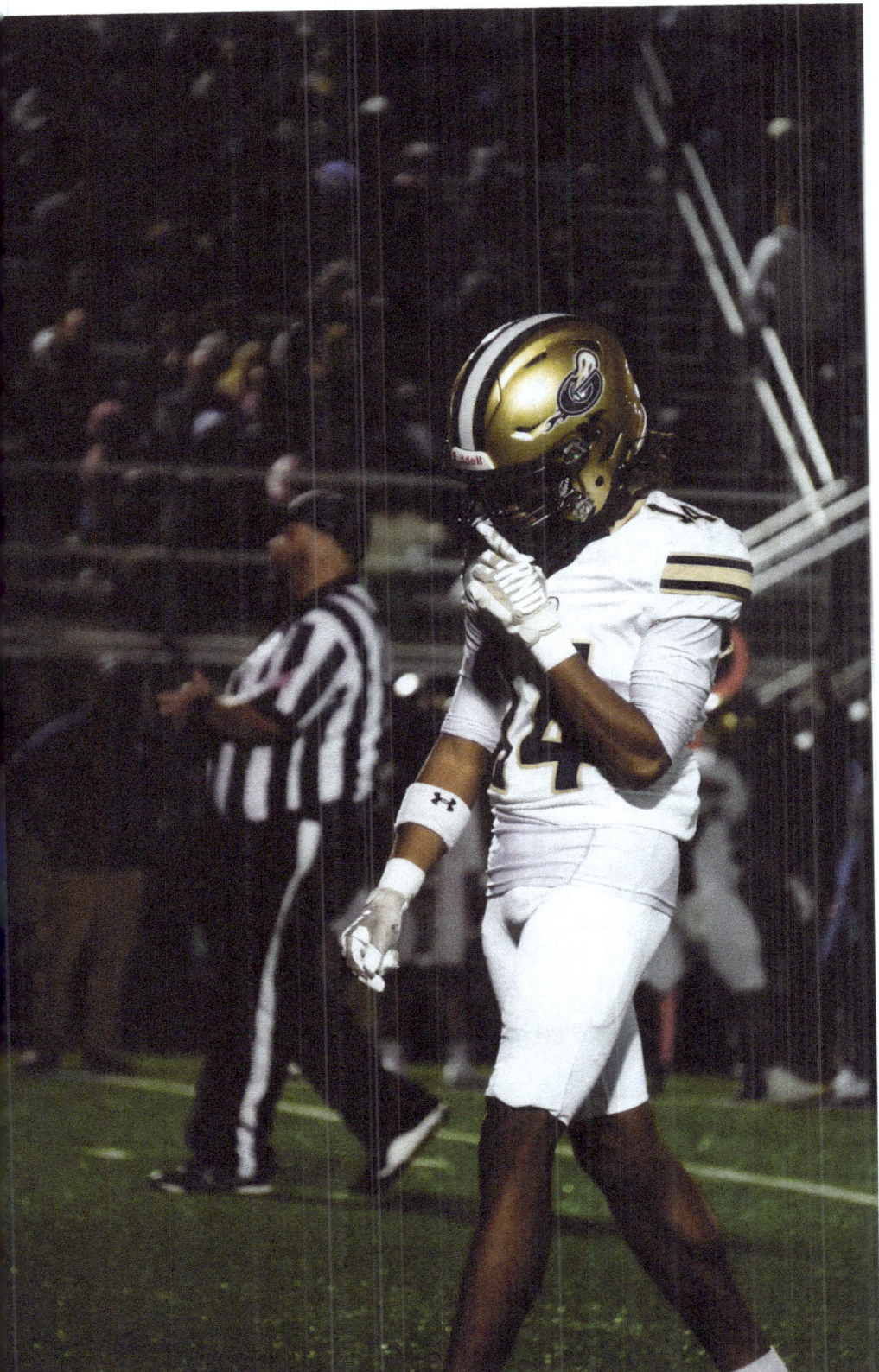

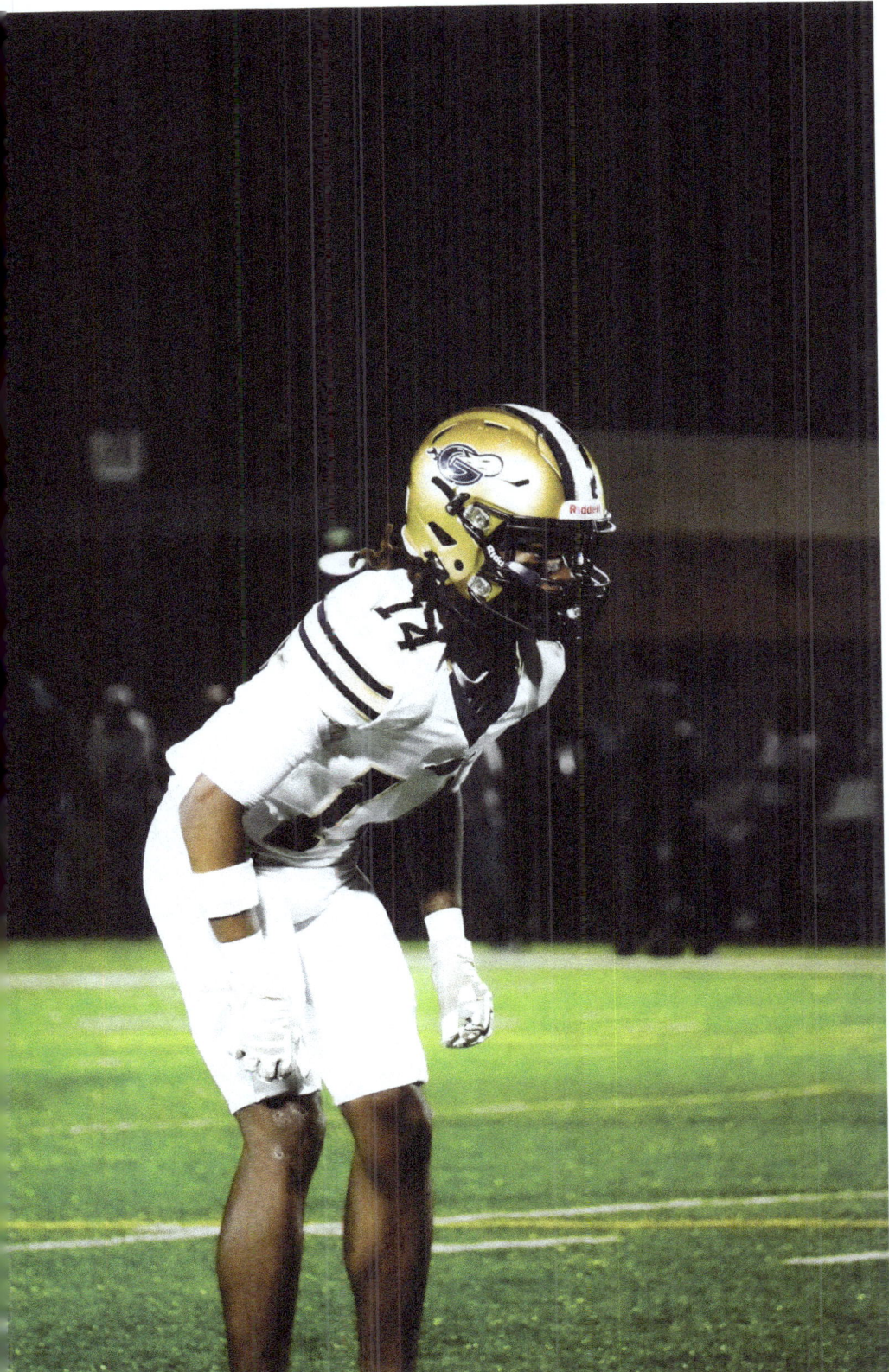

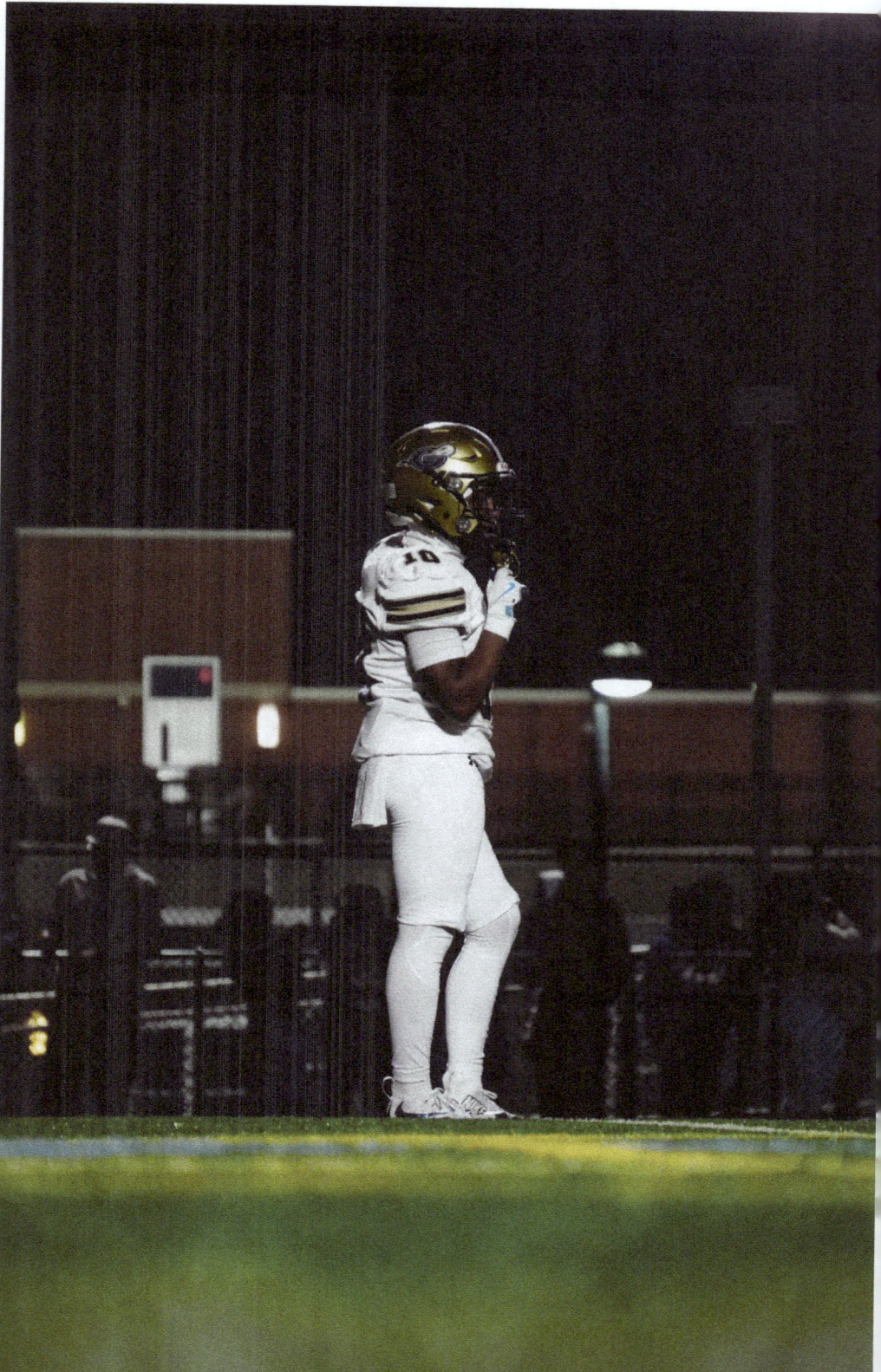

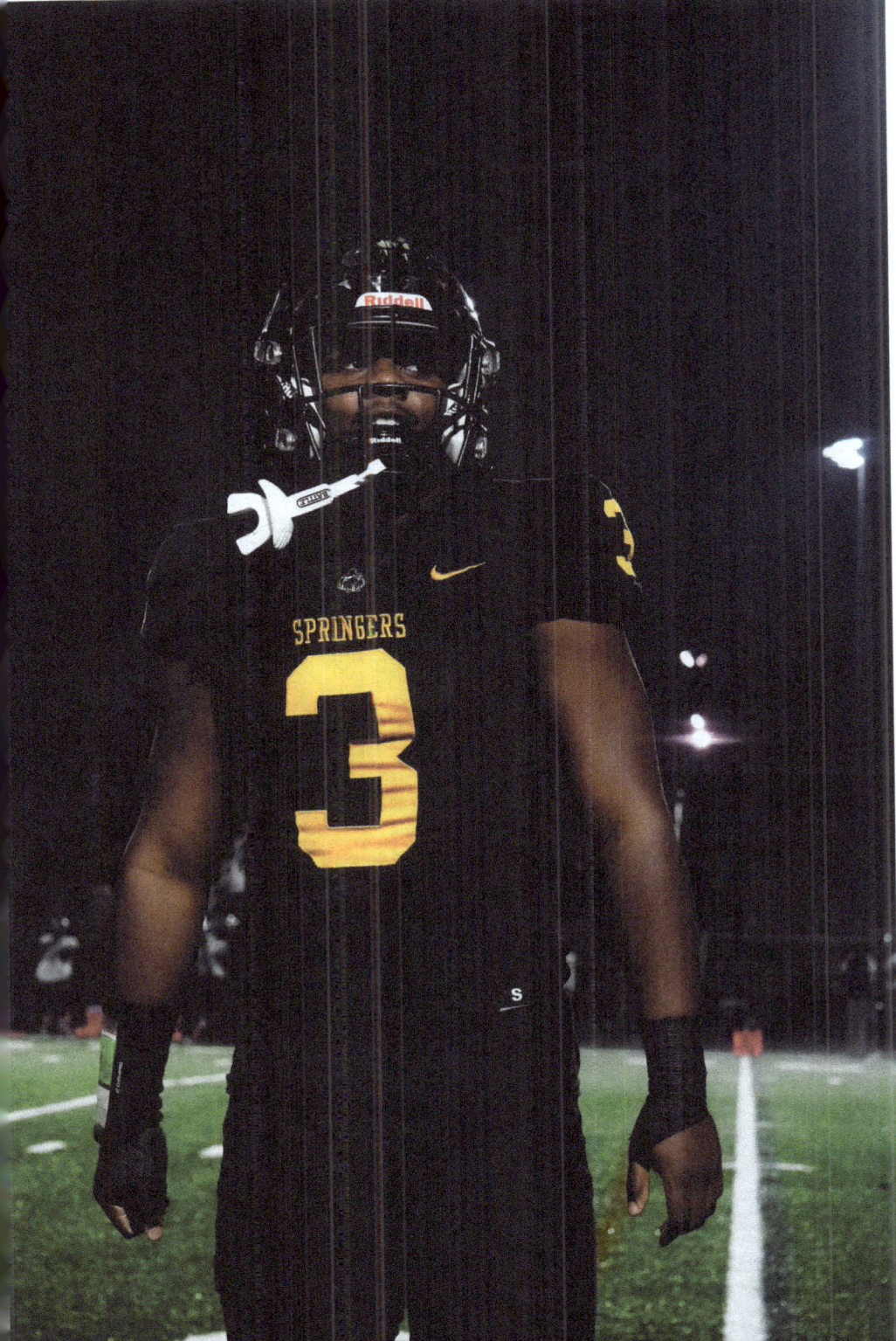

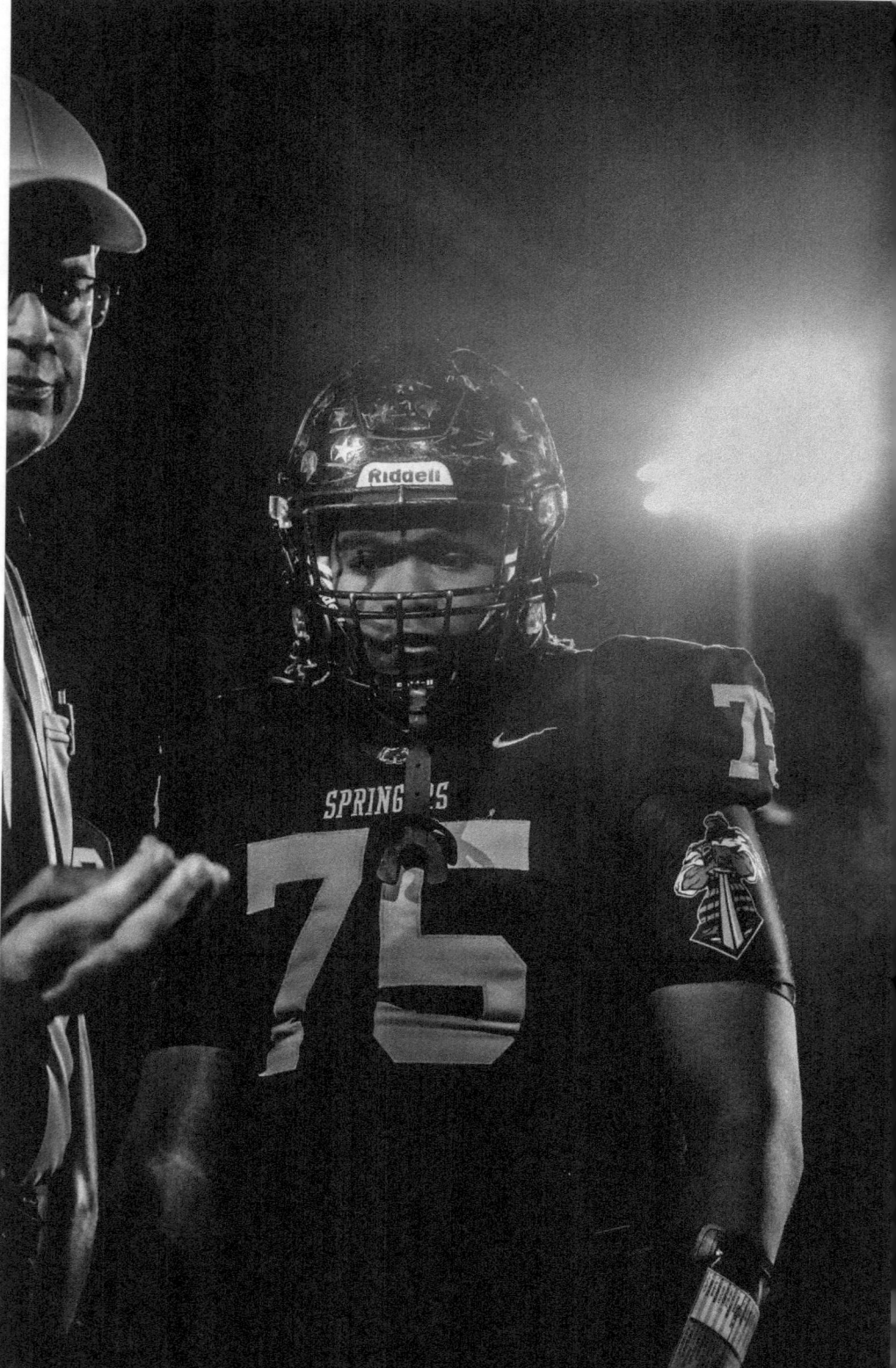

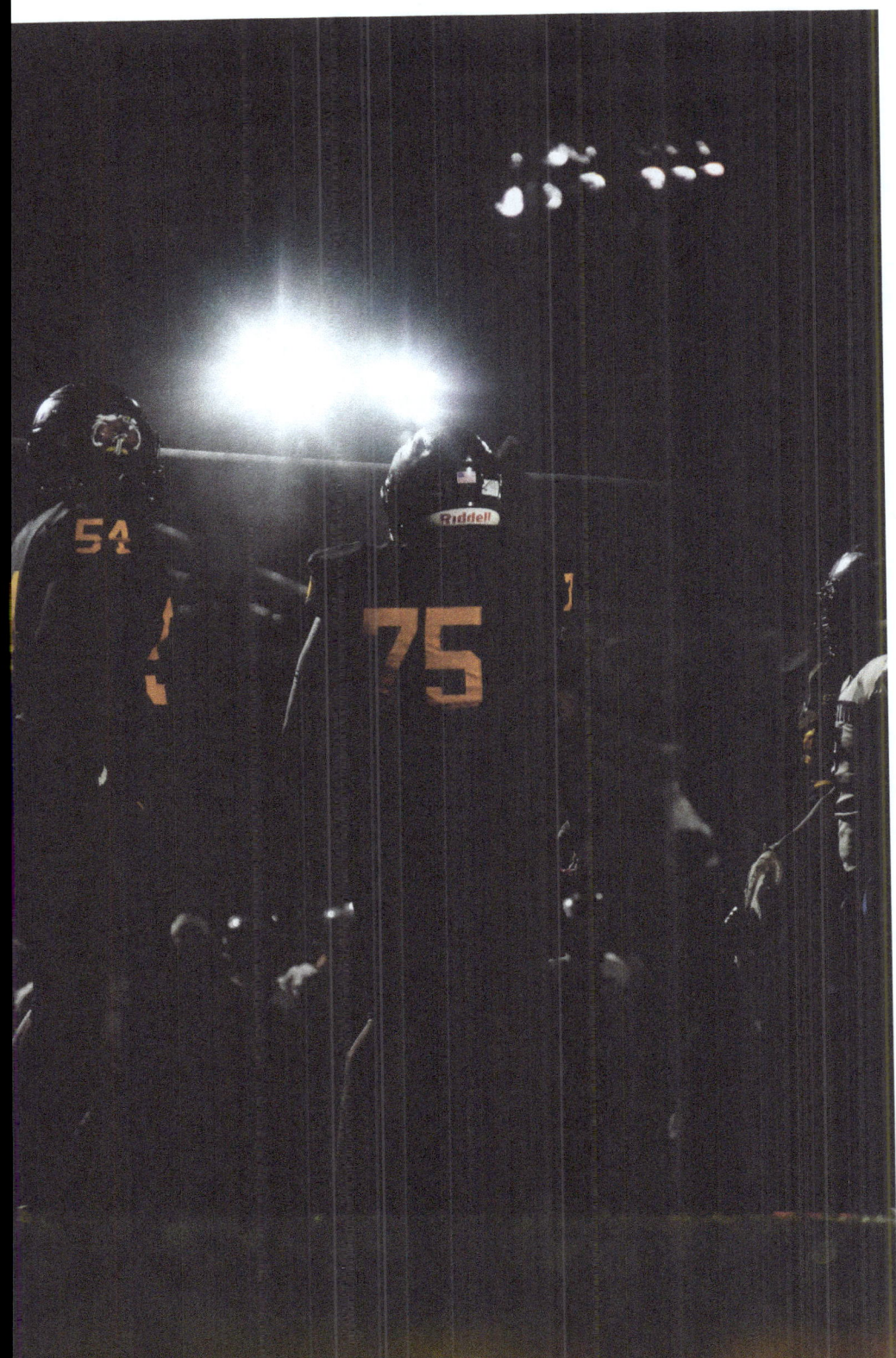

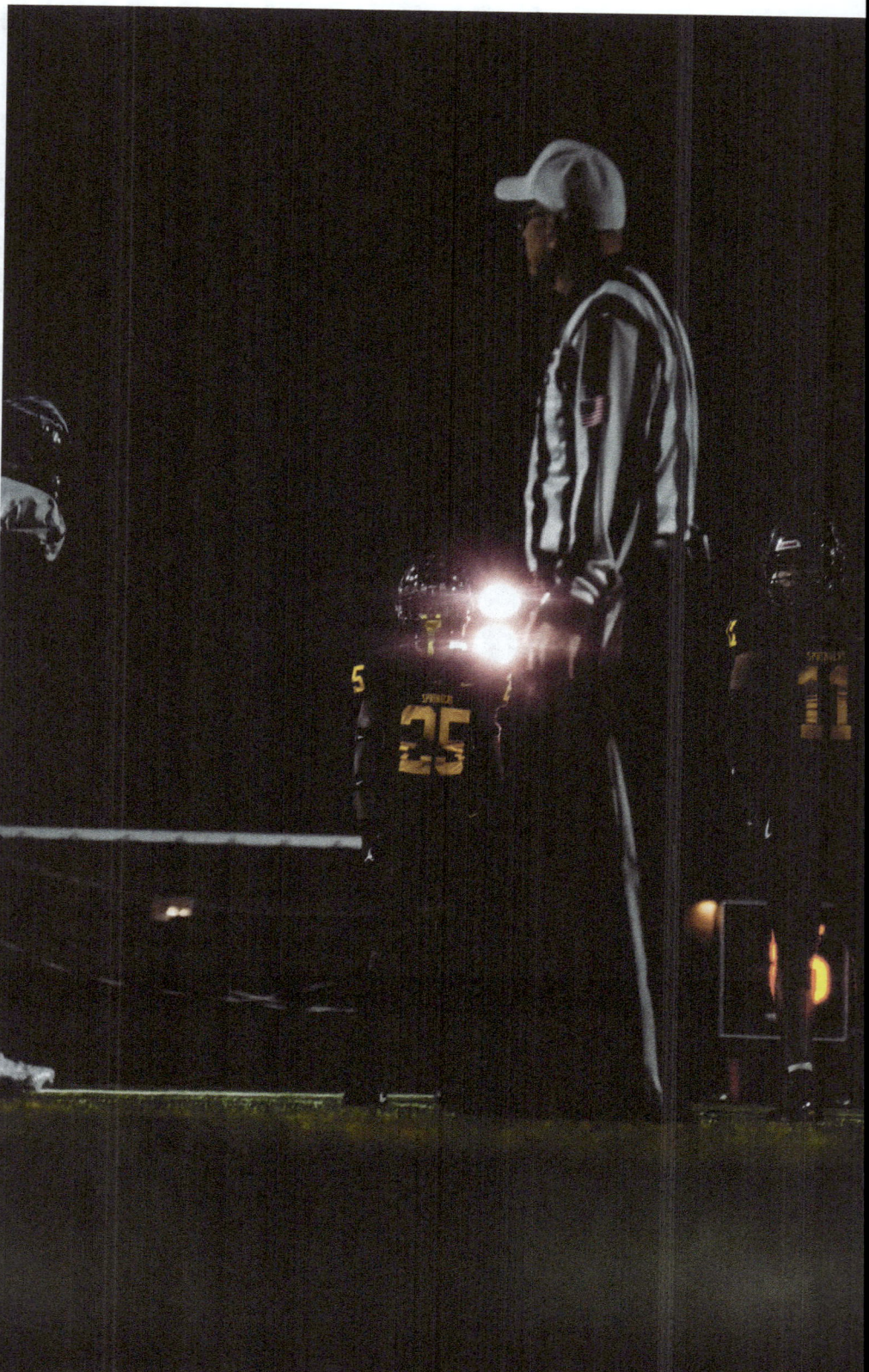

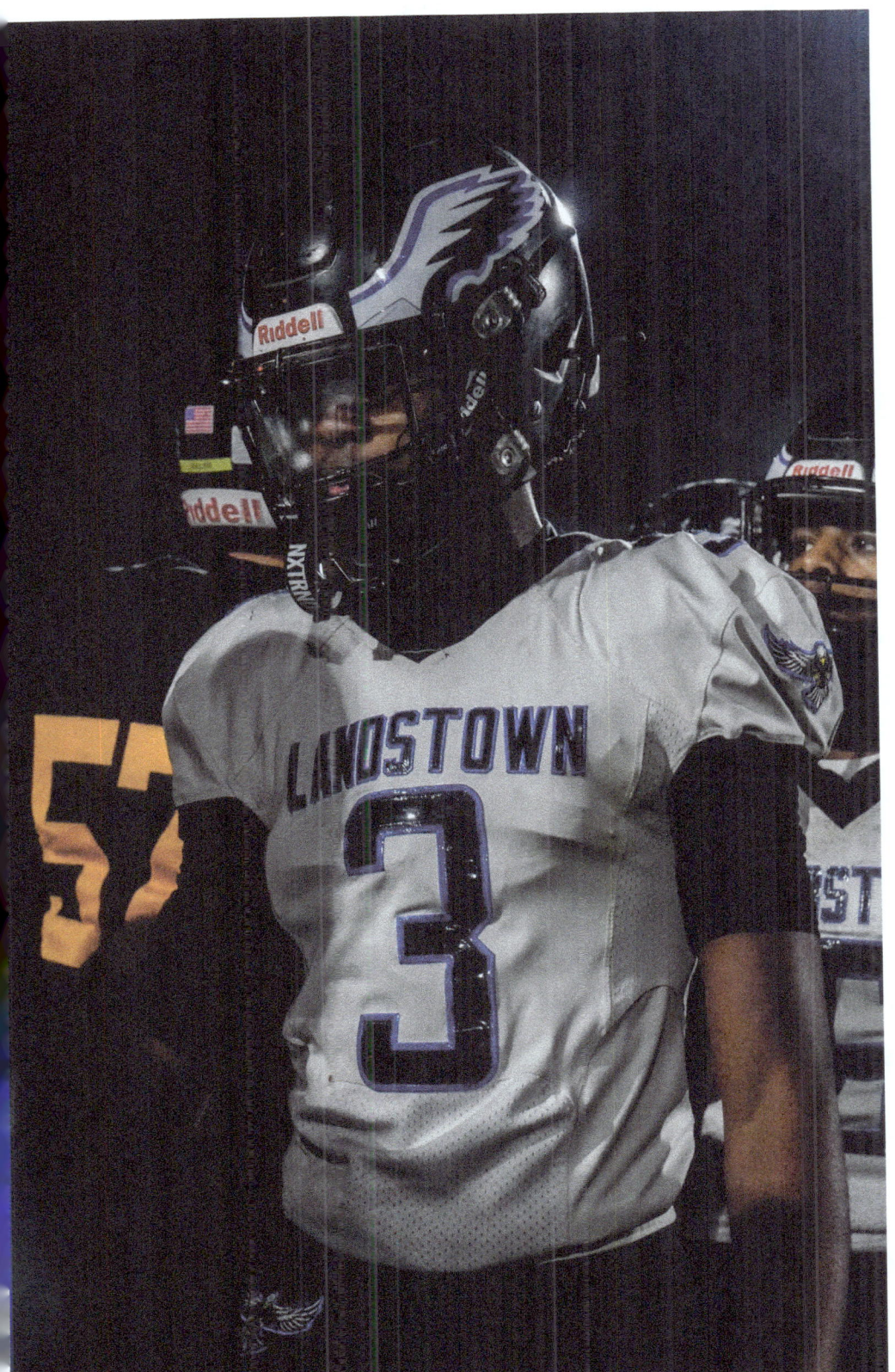

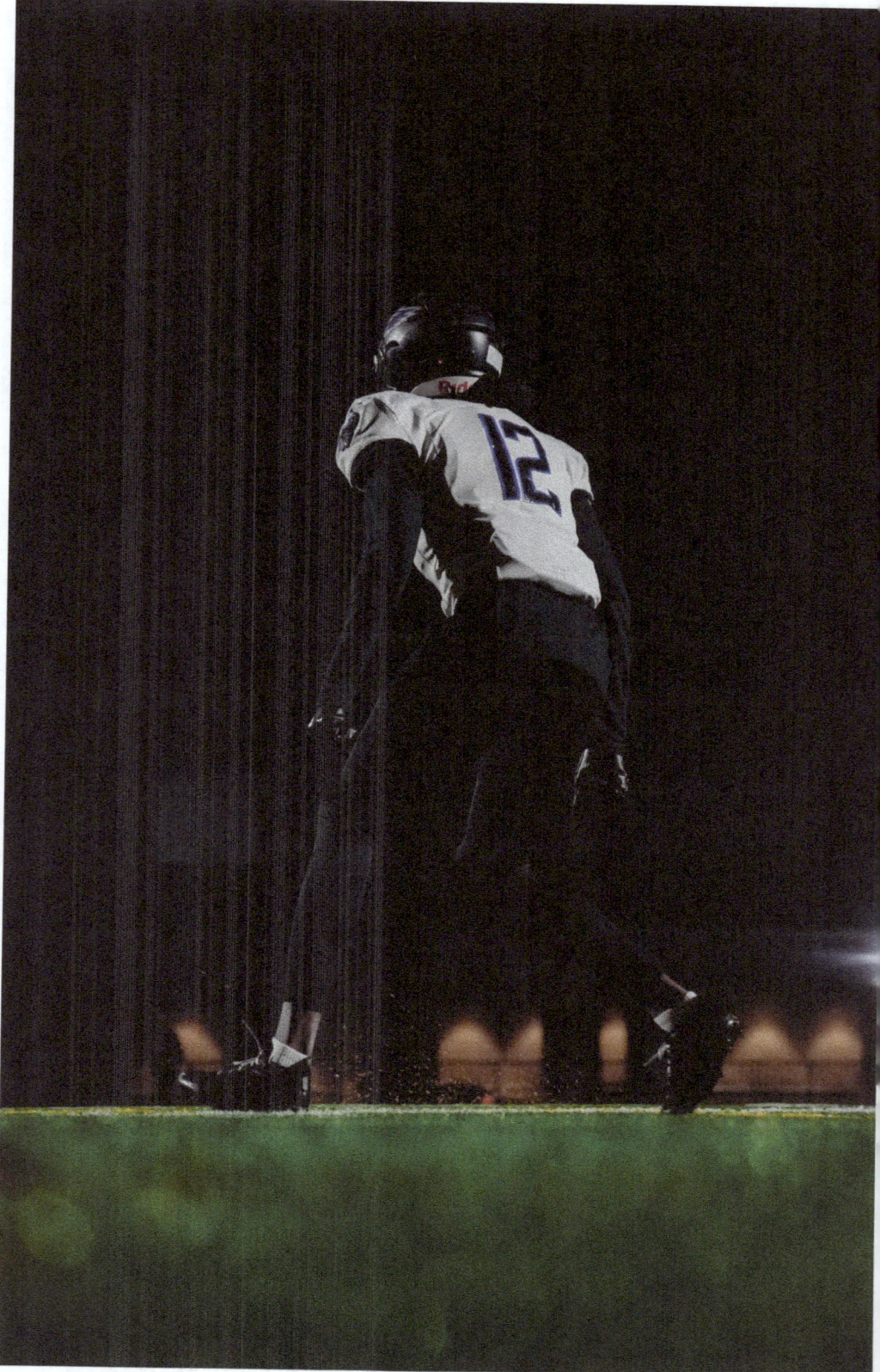

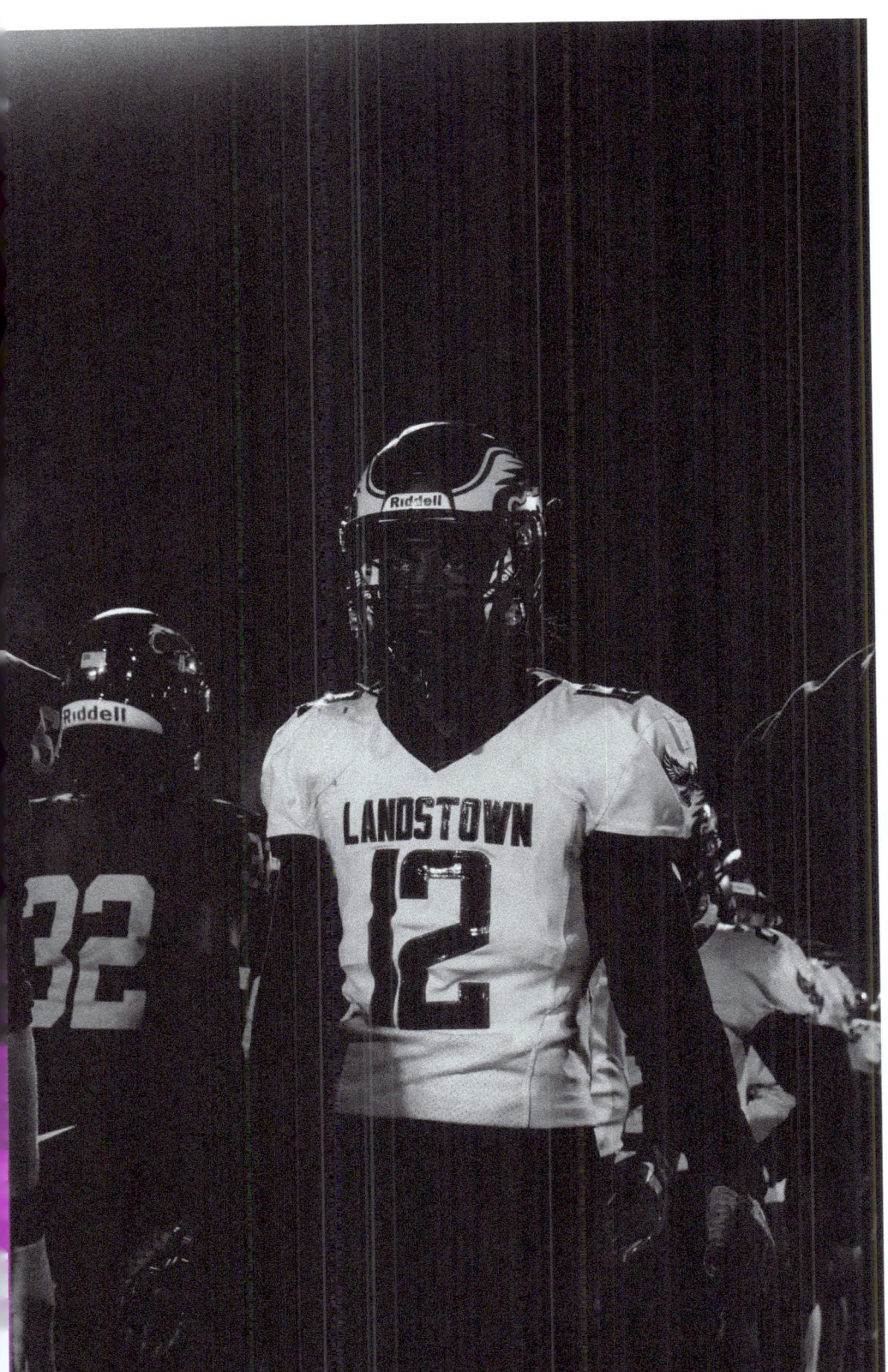

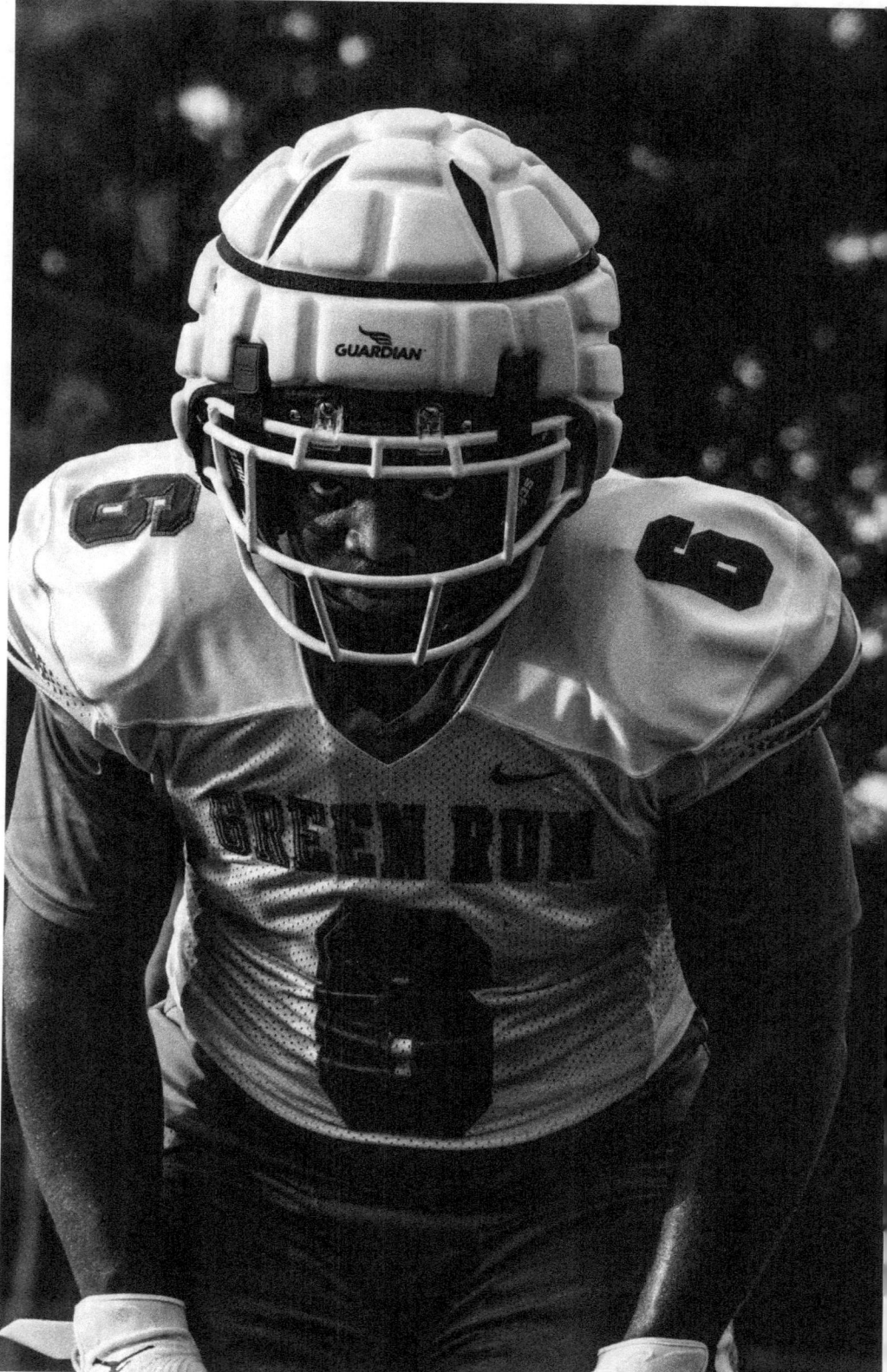

www.ingramcontent.com/pod-product-compliance
Lightning Source LLC
Chambersburg PA
CBHW070124230526
45472CB00004B/1413